Spiritual Care: A practical guide for nurses and health care practitioners, second edition

Aru Narayanasamy

Quay Books

Mark Allen
Publishing Ltd

1002951614

Quay Books Division, Mark Allen Publishing Limited
Jesses Farm, Snow Hill, Dinton, Wiltshire, SP3 5HN

British Library Cataloguing-in-Publication Data
A catalogue record is available for this book

© Mark Allen Publishing Ltd 2001
ISBN 1 85642 181 3

Printed in the UK by The Cromwell Press, Trowbridge, Wiltshire

Contents

Acknowledgement

My thanks to my wife, Mani for being a wise critic and supporter. My gratitude goes to: Ethelerene White for providing the material on Seventh Day Adventists; Steward Walker for the material on Jehovah's Witnesses and the University of Nottingham/Queen's Medical Centre for allowing extracts from the resource package *Spiritual, religious and Cultural Care* edited by Narayanasamy and Daly (1998) to be included in this book.

Introduction

Welcome to the second edition of this book which has been revised significantly to incorporate further material on spirituality and spiritual care. The primary purpose of this book has been retained to ensure that it continues to be a resource guide for nurses and health care practitioners who want a quick guided introduction to the subject of spirituality and spiritual care.

Nursing is primarily a service to humankind and this means a commitment to others. Serving others takes on a deeper dimension of loving and care as one promotes well-being. This involves the process in which spiritual resources of the nurses are shared with others. Within this lies the perspective of individuals being made up of the body, mind and spirit. Nursing must therefore strive to respond to the physical, emotional and spiritual needs of patients. However, there is evidence to suggest that the spiritual part of a person receives little attention in nursing (Narayanasamy, 1999). Millison (1988) asserts that spirituality is an underutilised facet of care. This book aims to heighten carers' awareness of spirituality and focuses on the much neglected areas of spirituality and spiritual care.

Where relevant, further guides to reading on the subject of spirituality are offered. *Chapter 1* offers the reader the opportunity to understand the term 'spirituality' in terms of a case illustration and activities related work. *Chapter 2* incorporates material on cultural dimensions of spirituality. It provides a model for cultural and spiritual dimensions of care as a tool for nursing patients from multi-cultural backgrounds. *Chapter 3* provides a focus on spiritual needs and the significance of certain spiritual needs during our development and growth. Religious needs are identified in *Chapter 4* together with guidance related to specific needs of patients from various faiths and backgrounds. It comprises further resource material on Humanism and Paganism. The need for certain skills development for spiritual care is stressed and explained in *Chapter 5*. *Chapter 6* takes the reader through the process of nursing in meeting the spiritual needs of patients. This chapter includes sections on assessment, planning, implementation and evaluation of spiritual care. In *Chapter 7*, several case histories are provided with corresponding nursing care plans outlined. The corresponding nursing care plans apply the nursing process to the case histories.

The final chapter makes reference to the emerging research related to spiritual care and acts as a good resource for readers looking for a starting point for research in this challenging and stimulating area of nursing.

References

Millison MB (1988) Spirituality and caregiver, developing an underutilised facet of care. *Am J Hospice Care*, March/April: 37–44

Narayanasamy A (1999) ASSET: A model for Actioning Spirituality and Spiritual Education and Training in Nursing. *Nurse Educ Today* **19**: 274–285

1

Spirituality

In this chapter spirituality is portrayed as an holistic dimension and as a necessary part of health care. Holistic approaches to health and health care require a holistic view of the individual. Many health carers claim that they have a commitment to holistic care; by this they usually mean care of the body, mind and spirit. However, the provision of spiritual care is less than ideal in practice. By implication, this claim that health care fully embraces holistic care is yet to be fully realised.

In a world dominated largely by secularism, today's focus tends to be on things that are orientated towards the present, materialistic, and tangible. It is not surprising that for many, spirituality is seen as something to do with religion, while others may attach very little importance to it. Concern for the spiritual aspects of a person (things that touch our inner core) is likely to receive less attention in our world dominated by technological advances and expectations of immediate results. However, religion is still active and well for many people and there is evidence to suggest that even in most secular countries, there is a revival in the spiritual side of life (Reid, 1992). Human life is governed by social, psychological, physical and spiritual influences. If we as health care professionals are to accept that spiritual aspects of a person are just as important as social, psychological and physical dimensions of life, then we must pay serious attention to beliefs and practices that govern individuals.

Spiritual beliefs and practices permeate the life of a person, whether in health or illness. Certain spiritual needs tend to feature during our personal development and growth (to be discussed later). Spirituality and religion are so pervasive that their influences can be seen in almost all aspects of people's lives: relationships with others, life style and habits; required and prohibited behaviours; and the general frame of reference for thinking about oneself and the world. As mentioned earlier, our spirituality features during our development and growth.

In nursing and health care a focus on the notion of the totality of the person as encompassing body, mind and spirit is gaining recognition, but there is little elaboration on what is meant by spirit.

This problem is further compounded by the misuse of the term spirituality, in that this word is equated to, or is applied synonymously with, institutional religion. Institutional religions usually refer (for example, in the United Kingdom at least) to Christianity, Islam, Judaism, Hinduism, Sikhism and Buddhism.

Spirituality and religion

What is spirituality?

There is no single authoritative definition of spirituality, although a variety of explanations are offered in the emerging literature. As seen earlier, when we refer to 'holistic approach' we mean care of the body, mind and spirit. Holistic care is a popular concept in nursing and health care, and there are ample theories on this in the literature, but spirituality as an aspect of nursing is given little weight. A clear grasp of the concept of spirituality is required if we are going to offer it as a component of holistic care.

Although there is an overlap between spirituality, ethics, psychology, sociology, politics and so on, it should be seen as a distinct discipline with developing sets of theories. You may find that religious needs and spirituality are closely connected, and sometimes find it difficult to make the distinction between them as one need affects the other.

Activity one

Spend a few minutes thinking about the concept of spirituality, and then write below what you mean by the term 'spirituality'?

Feedback on activity one

When you tried to think about spirituality, perhaps you conjured up several concepts in your mind. Your written responses may have included examples like those produced by members on a spiritual care course:

❖ Beliefs affecting one's life and how it relates to others.

❖ Something not necessarily religious.

❖ Purpose and meaning of life.

❖ A source of strength.

❖ At peace with oneself.

❖ Inner peace.

❖ A feeling of security.

❖ Love and to be loved.

❖ Self-esteem.

❖ Inner self.

❖ Inner strength.

❖ Searching.

❖ Coping.

❖ Hope and security.

❖ Trusting relationship.

❖ Connectedness.

Spirituality is usually a much more abstract concept than religion and includes areas such as the meaning of life, love, humanity, inner peace, tranquillity, meditation, relationships, individuality, personal worth and so on. For many people, it is private and refers to their inner self and there may be a reticence to talk openly about it. Spirituality may be viewed as a subjective dimension, implicit in nature, inward and to do with feelings and experiences, a personal entity and a form of journey. These will be discussed in detail later in this chapter.

History suggests that since the beginning of humanity spirituality has always featured in people's lives in some way or another. Spirituality is one of the fashionable words in nursing, yet like so many useful and comprehensive terms, it is elusive and not easy to define. You probably arrived at a similar conclusion from the activity you have just completed.

Spirituality can be defined as:

> *Spirituality is rooted in an awareness which is part of the biological make up of the human species. Spirituality is present in all individuals and it may manifest as inner peace and strength derived from a perceived relationship with a transcendent God/an ultimate reality, or whatever an individual values as supreme.*
>
> *The spiritual dimension evokes feelings which demonstrate the existence of love, faith, hope, trust, awe, inspirations; therein providing meaning and a reason for existence. It comes into focus particularly when an individual faces emotional stress, physical illness or death.*
>
> Narayanasamy, 1999

Religion

Activity two

Consider for a few minutes what you mean by religion, and then write below your responses.

Feedback on activity two

Some people draw only small differences between the meaning of 'religion' and 'spirituality', but most people identify many significant differences:

❖ Belief in God; a supreme being, transcendent, ultimate reality, someone divine and so on.

❖ Structures and institutions: churches; cathedrals; temples; mosques; places of worship.

❖ Doctrines, religious laws, rules, codes of practice, etc.

❖ Church hierarchy, clergy, spiritual leaders, prophets, the Pope, gurus, etc.

❖ Symbols and icons, The Cross, Holy books, the Bible, Koran, Gita, etc.

❖ Ceremonies and rituals: birth, puberty, marriage and deaths.

❖ Holy songs and music;

❖ Fundamentalism, conflicts, crusades, etc.

The word religion tends to create images in our minds of external things like buildings, religious officials and public rituals, such as circumcisions, baptisms, weddings or funerals. For some individuals these are the times when they come into contact with something to do with religion, with or without a deeper religious significance. Murray and Zentner (1989) define religion as:

> *A belief in a supernatural or divine force that has power over the universe and commands worship and obedience; a system of beliefs; a comprehensive code of ethics or philosophy; a set of practices that are followed; a church affiliation; the conscious pursuit of any object the person holds as supreme.*
>
> p. 259

In contrast to spirituality which is implicit, inward and to do with feelings and experience, religion is seen as a concrete dimension that is explicit and outward, related to objective things like institutions. For some people religion is a mode of transport for their spiritual journey.

Spirituality as a universal dimension

There is something universal about the spiritual dimension and the capacity to experience spirituality belongs to all of us. As depicted in the definition (Narayanasamy, 1999) given on *page 4*, even the non-religious person exhibits something of the serenity and inward peace which are especially characteristic of those who tend to be outwardly religious.

The something that drives and motivates us to make sense of the meaningless world that we are born into is our spiritual dimension. According to Macquarie (1972) the spiritual person is one who has made sense of the meaningless world and has learned to be at home in the universe by deriving a certain serenity and inward peace. This assumption leads to the belief that people in their endeavour to make sense of their world have developed this extra dimension, that is spirituality. As part of the search for meaning, some people try to find answers to the irrational and meaningless world through religious faith. This includes spirituality as embracing spiritual life and its activities such as prayer, worship and whatever practices are associated with its development.

Writing from an existential perspective Macquarie (1972) provides some understanding on spirituality. He suggests that our motivation for seeking meaning and purpose renders us as distinct beings, setting us apart from other physical organisms. In other words we, as individuals, are made up of the body, mind and spirit. In regard to this Macquarie writes:

> *We do not relate to other people as if they were only objects that we could see and hear and touch or even as if they were simply living organisms from which reactions could be evoked. We relate to them as persons, and we talk about them or talk to them in a language appropriate to persons. What makes the difference between a person and an animal is not itself something that is to be seen. It is the inevitable 'extra dimension'... . It is this range of experience that is distinctive of the human being and that we call 'spirit'.*

p.46

Macquarie implies that an individual becomes a spiritual person when one has made sense of this meaningless world and has learned to be adaptable by deriving a certain serenity and inward peace. Macquarie's position on spirituality strengthens the assertion in nursing that spirituality is an holistic notion.

Spirituality as an holistic notion

An idealistic view exists in health care that spirituality is an holistic notion in the sense that an individual is made up of the body, mind and spirit, and that these components are interconnected and inter-dependent (Stallwood, 1981; Carson, 1989; Shelly and Fish, 1988). The word 'holism', gained popularity following the work of Jan Christian Smuts (1926), a South African philosopher and politician, who introduced it in the early part of the twentieth century. Holism relates to the study of whole organism or whole system, its spelling derived from the Greek word 'holos' meaning 'whole'. In applying it to the Western health care context, it may be seen as an approach that incorporates the interrelationships between all aspects of bodily functions and psycho-social functions in a sort of multifaceted approach to the human being.

Holism in both senses means that there is now a drift from the ideas proposed by Descartes who claimed that, in order to study the body as a machine, it could be broken down into its components parts (Bradshaw, 1994). If holism is accepted in terms of the above perspectives, then there is a need to view a person as a whole being, and the manner in which the body, mind and spirit interact.

In considering spirituality as an holistic notion in nursing, Stallwood (1981) illustrates its holistic features in her conceptual model of the nature of a person (*Figure 1.1*). Stallwood is not implying dualism as described by the philosopher, Descartes who saw the body, mind and spirit as distinct and independent entities. Stallwood explains that an individual as an integrated whole is made up of the body, mind (psycho-social) and spirit, and that these components are dynamically woven together, one part affecting and being affected by the other parts. *Figure 1.1* depicts an adaptation of a model developed by Stall-wood as an illustration of a person's wholeness.

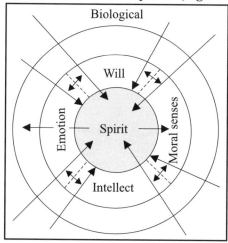

Figure 1.1: Conceptual nature of a person

The human person is and functions as a dynamic whole. This is depicted in the model by the broken lines and arrows. The biological dimension influences and is influenced by the psychosocial dimension of the person expressed itself through the body. The spirit expresses itself through the total being – the psychosocial and biological dimensions.

On the other hand, Gorham (1989) offers a five component person model which could be applied to anyone in ill health. This model depicts a person as being made up of five of different aspects – the mental, the physical, the social, the emotional, and the spiritual. The interaction is so closely related that they are almost inseparable. The spiritual dimension is the most difficult one to be recognised. The interactions of these five components are illustrated in *Figure 1.2*.

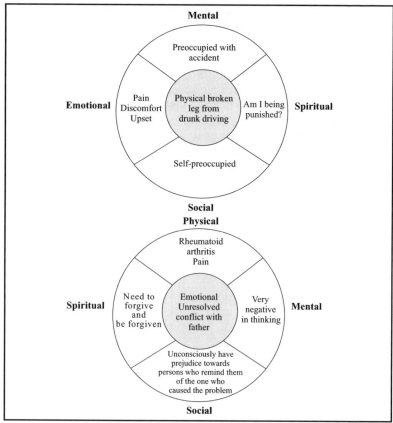

Figure 1.2: The five-component person model

The two models of spirituality in *Figure 1.2* demonstrate the holistic nature of this concept.

Evidence is emerging in the nursing literature that spirituality is seen as an all embracing dimension. In developing the holistic notion of health nursing theorists have described spirituality as:

* the process of a sacred journey (Mische, 1982)
* the essence or life principle of a person (Collinton, 1981)
* the experience of the radical truth of things (Legere, 1984)
* a belief that relates a person to the world (Soeken and Carson, 1987)
* giving meaning and purpose in life (Legere, 1984)
* a life relationship or a sense of connection with mystery, Higher Power, God or Universe (Granstrom, 1985).

However, there are criticisms of the holistic perspective of spirituality. Hay (1987; 1994) implies that this view is not comprehensive enough in that the present holistic approach does not include the biological basis of spirituality. Hay's views on this in the light of emerging research are explained next. The evidence from research studies (Hay, 1994; 1987; Hardy, 1979) suggests that spirituality is an innate biological dimension which frequently emerges during personal crises. Writing from a biological perspective, Hay and Hardy view spirituality in the sense of spiritual awareness and experiences, ie. the Numinous (James, 1902; Stace, 1960) and Mystical States (Otto, 1950). That is, being aware of oneself in an holistic relationship with rest of reality, which in religious experience implies an awareness of God or Divinity.

Using the evolutionary theory they hypothesise that spiritual awareness is an innate thing and that it is a universal and everlasting phenomenon because of its survival value. In the light of their research findings related to people's experience of spiritual awareness they postulate that this has been necessary for the survival of the human species through the natural process of evolution.

Although Hay and Hardy use the concept of spirituality inter-changeably with religion, their studies have generated interesting findings. National surveys (Hardy, 1979; Hay, 1987) suggest a trend that about half of the British adult population would claim that they are spiritually or religiously aware, from time to time. Hay (1994) suggests that further in-depth studies boost this figure to about two thirds when there is the opportunity to build trust; that is, when respondents feel confident to trust others to reveal their personal and private experiences. This was borne out by the findings of a study (Narayanasamy, 1995) on the 'Spiritual care of chronically ill patients', where patients' trust in the interviewer prompted them to reveal intimate details about their spirituality and spiritual concerns.

Interestingly, Hay (1987) suggests that the evidence from comparative religions is that literally anything or any occasion can be associated with a sudden moment of religious awareness. Records of individual's accounts exist of such moments 'during childbirth, at the point of death, during sexual intercourse, at a meal, during fasting, in a Cathedral, on a rubbish dump, on a mountain top, in a slum, in association with a particular plant, stone, fish, mammal, bird and so on and infinitum' (Hay, 1987, p. 207). In a way this is akin to Laski's (1961) suggestion that there are special 'triggers' for experiencing spiritual awareness that are mystical in nature. However, it appears that secular cultures tend to teach us to associate transcendental experience with particular occasions and place. Research studies (Hay, 1987) have consistently suggested that people who claim to have undergone spiritual experience appear to be:

* calmer and stable
* able to find meaning in their lives
* concerned with issues of social justice
* tolerant of others
* less materialistic
* less status conscious
* less likely than others to be racially prejudiced.

Although the theories examined so far differ somewhat in the way that spirituality is viewed, there appears to be common understanding that spirituality is seen as an inner thing that is central to the person's being, making a person unique and 'tick over' as an individual. For example, I see it as my being; my inner person. It is who I am, unique and alive. It is expressed through my body, my thinking, my feelings, my judgements, and my creativity. My spirituality motivates me to choose meaningful relationships and pursuits.

Sometimes we desire for personal quest for meaning and purpose in life: a sense of harmonious relationships (interconnectedness) with self and others, nature, an ultimate other, and other factors which are necessary for our integrity. These points can be illustrated in the case of Elsie below.

Activity three

Read the case illustration and try to identify elements of Elsie's spirituality below.

Case illustration

Elsie looks after her elderly mother who is an invalid and has been a widow for the last ten years. She feels that it is her duty to care for her mother who is totally dependent on her. Elsie frequently says to the community nurse that it has not always been an easy task, but she learnt a lot in the last 10 years through caring for her mother, and she has become more appreciative of the beauty and joy in life. Elsie sees each day as a new opportunity to learn and grow. The community nurse feels that in Elsie's presence she experiences a sense of peace and who, even in the midst of difficult and trying circumstances, affirms that life is good. Elsie says that she has done some soul-searching over the last ten years and has come to know herself pretty well. She states to the nurses that when she felt low, she learned to 'go inside herself' and always finds guidance there and achieves a sense of relief and comfort. She also adds that she maintains a close relationship with family and friends with whom she shares love and support. Elsie is a keen gardener and when in her garden she feels close to the earth and to the Creator.

Feedback from activity

Several of the elements of spirituality can be illustrated in the case of Elsie:

❖ Unfolding mystery: through life's 'ups and downs' and what could be viewed as a burden, she has found meaning and joy.

❖ Inner strength: she has developed a great sense of self-awareness, which she has gained by going inside herself (a process also known as introspection) for guidance.

❖ Harmonious interconnectedness: she has loving, supporting relationships with family and friends, a sense of knowing herself.

❖ Source of strength and hope: the garden has become a place where she is able to express a feeling of closeness to nature and the Creator.

It appears that spirituality is essential to our well-being and is the essence of our existence. It has to do with both solitude and corporate life including the way we think, act and feel in every day life. In essence, we can now see that it influences the whole of our lives. As seen earlier, people who do not have recourse to God or religion are also spiritual beings (see 'Agnosticism and atheism', below).

Furthermore, through our spirituality we give and receive love. We respond by appreciating God, other people, a sunset, a symphony, or spring. Many of us keep our spirits up in spite of adversity and it may well be because something motivates us to do so. This is because of spirituality. Elsie's situation is a good example of spirituality as it keeps her going in spite of all the odds. We are driven forward, sometimes because of pain, sometimes in spite of pain. Spirituality permits a person to function, to be motivated and able to value, worship, and communicate with the holy, the transcendent.

Transcendence is as much a personal need as are physiological or psychological requirements. If we take this view, then we as nurses and health carers should regard all individuals as spiritual beings and not as a body with just physiological and psychological needs.

Agnosticism and atheism

Atheists and agnostics are spiritual beings. Atheists do not believe in a supreme being, life after death, or any Divine plan for humanity, whereas agnostics hold that the existence of anything beyond material phenomena cannot be known and that the truth can only be determined by reason or scientific evidence (Narayanasamy and Daly, 1998).

Spiritual well-being

After this discussion of spirituality, let us look at the concept of spiritual well-being. Please attempt activity four below.

Activity four

Consider for a few minutes what you mean by spiritual well-being, and then write below your responses.

Spiritual well-being is an important facet of health and is considered to be an affirmation of our relationship with God/Transcendent, self, community and environment that nurtures and keeps us as an integrated whole person. Features of our spiritual well-being are:

* the belief in God that is fostered through communication with the Supreme Being; expression of love, concern, and forgiveness for others
* giving and accepting help
* accepting and valuing of self
* expressing life satisfaction.

Furthermore, our spiritual well-being is usually demonstrated by our ability to find meaning and purpose in present life situations and to search for meaning and purpose in the future. It is also a state of harmonious relationship between self, others/nature, and an ultimate other that is enduring throughout life and extends beyond time and space. We can attain spiritual well-being through a dynamic and integrative growth process which leads to a realisation of the ultimate purpose and meaning in life.

Conclusion

Clearly, there is no one single authoritative definition of spirituality, although some authors have attempted to define it in broader terms. Spirituality refers to a broader dimension that is sometimes beyond the realm of subjective explanation. It is an inspirational expression as a reaction to a religious force or an abstract philosophy as defined by the individual. It is a quality that is present in believers, and even in atheists and agnostics, provided that there is the opportunity to feel and express this inspirational experience according to the individual's own understanding of this phenomenon. In the next chapter the significance of spirituality and culture is explored and explained.

References

Bradshaw A (1994). *Lighting the Lamp: The Spiritual Dimension of Nursing Care*. Scutari Press, London

Carson VB (1989). *Spiritual Dimensions of Nursing Practice*. B Saunders Company, Philadelphia

Collinton M (1981). 'The spiritual dimension of nursing'. In Bell E, Passos JY (eds) *Clinical Nursing*. Macmillan, New York

Gorham (1989) Spirituality and problems solving with seniors. *Perspectives* **13**(3): 13–16

Granstrom SL (1985). Spiritual Nursing Care for Oncology Patients. *Top Clin Nurs* **7**(1): 39–45

Hardy A (1979) *The Spiritual Nature of Man*. Clarendon Press, Oxford

Hay D (1987) *Exploring Inner Space: Scientist and Religious Experience*. Mowbray, London

Hay D (1994). On the biology of God: What is the current status of Hardy's hypothesis? *Int J Psychol Religion* **4**(1): 1–23

James W (1902) *The Varieties of Religious Experience*. The Fontana Library, New York

Laski M (1961) *Ecstacy*. The Cresset Press, London

Legere T (1984) A spirituality for today. *Stud Formative Spirituality* **5**(3): 375–385

Macquarie J (1972) *Existentialism*. Penguin, Harmondsworth

Mische P (1982) Toward a global spirituality. In: Mische P (ed) *Whole Earth Papers*. Global Education Association, East Grange, NJ: No 16

Murray R, Zentner JP (1989) *Nursing Concepts for Health Promotion*. Prentice Hall, London

Narayanasamy A (1995) Research in brief: spiritual care of chronic ill patients. *J Clin Nurs* **5**(7): 411–16

Narayanasamy A, Daly P (1998) *Spiritual, Religious and Cultural Care: A Resource Package*. Queens Medical Centre, Nottingham

Narayanasamy A (1999) A review of spirituality as applied to nursing. *Int J Nurs Stud* **36**: 117–25

Otto R (1950) *The Idea of the Holy*. University Press, Oxford

Reid G (1992) The spiritual dimension. In: Keely R (ed) *Introduction to the Christian Faith*. Lynx Communication, Oxford:18–22

Shelley AL, Fish S (1988) *Spiritual Care: The Nurses Role* .Inter Varsity Press, East Grange, NJ

Smuts JC (1926) *Holism and Evolution*. Macmillan, New York

Soeken KL, Carson VJ (1987) Responding to the spiritual needs of the chronically ill. *Nurs Clin North Am* **22**(3): 603–11

Stace WT (1960) *Mysticism and Philosophy*. Lippincott, London

Stallwood J (1981) Spiritual Dimensions of Nursing Practice. In: Bell IL, Passos JY (eds) *Clinical Nursing*. Macmillan, New York

Annotated bibliographies

Readers wishing to explore further the concept of spirituality may find the the following useful.

Bradshaw A (1994) *Lighting the Lamp: the spiritual dimension of nursing care*. Scutari Press, London

This book provides a comprehensive review of the spiritual dimension and in-depth discussion on the history and theology of spirituality. Some of the points raised in the book would be useful material for the debate in this subject.

Carson VB (1989) *Spiritual Dimensions of Nursing Practice*. WB Saunders, London

The concept of spirituality is adequately treated in chapter one of this book. The development of spirituality in individuals is explored in chapter two. Both chapters provide sufficient material for readers wishing to gain a good understanding of the concept of spirituality.

McSherry W (2000) *Making Sense of Spirituality in Nursing Practice*. Churchill Livingstone, Edinburgh

The author of this book states that holistic care should embrace all aspects of humanity, including the spiritual dimension. In recognition of this, it aims to provide a practical interactive resource on spirituality for students and qualified nurses. Throughout, the book attempts to engage the reader in their quest for increasing their understanding of spirituality and spiritual care which is at times considered to be a difficult and nebulous subject for lack of clarity as to what it actually is. There are seven chapters in the book and each chapter explores a particular topic related to the theme of the book with much interactive activity-based tasks for readers, and ends with some selective commentaries on reading material for readers wishing to pursue this further.

Narayanasamy A (1999) A review of spirituality as applied to nursing. *Int J Nurs Stud* **36**: 117–125

Readers wishing to explore the experiential and biological perspectives of spirituality may find this paper worthwhile. This paper offers a review of spirituality as applied to nursing. It provides in-depth analysis of the holistic perspectives of spirituality as applied in nursing. It also brings to readers' attention the emerging empirical research in this area of humanity. The definition of spirituality offered in this chapter is derived from this paper.

Ronaldson S (ed) (1997) *Spirituality: The Heart of Nursing*. Alismed Publications, Melbourne

This book addresses many issues central to spirituality and nursing care. A range of spiritual care as practised in a variety of settings is presented from the perspectives of leading academics and clinicians in Australia. In particular, readers will find chapters on spirituality valuable.

Shelly JA, Fish S (1988) *Spiritual Care: The Nurses Role*. Inter Varsity Press, Illinois

Although written from a Christian perspective, readers will find useful sections which explore the concept of spirituality. Chapters one to three are particularly useful and assist the reader to 'grasp' the concept of spirituality. The book also includes a workbook section that contains individual exercises for developing spiritual awareness.

2

Spirituality and culture

Introduction

This chapter explores the cultural dimensions of spirituality. The ways in which individuals experience and practise their spirituality may depend upon their cultural roots and upbringing. Consideration and sensitivity is required when caring for patients from multi-cultural and religious backgrounds. As pointed out in *Chapter 1*, believers find that their religions are important media for expressing their spirituality. Some people, as members of a multicultural British society, reflect these cultural variations in the way that they practise their religions. Their spiritual needs often reflect these cultural variations, may be in terms of Western or Eastern cultures.

Western spirituality

Western spirituality is perceived to be based on the traditions of Judaism or Christianity. In Christianity and Judaism, spirituality is viewed as a theistic notion from the classical theological perspective. Theology has traditionally been defined as knowledge of God. In other words, it was used for the disciplined study which explores God, his nature, his attributes and his relations with the universe and people. Christian theology is embedded in a belief that God reveals himself in nature and history and human affairs (Brown, 1993; Bradshaw, 1994). In Judaism and Christianity theism refers to beliefs in God and monotheism refers to beliefs in one God.

In the nursing literature on spirituality, Bradshaw (1994) uses the classical theological explanation to tell us about the disclosure of God in the person of Christ. In developing the theological explanation Bradshaw puts forward that the place of man and woman (humanity) in the creation is as the image of God. Man and woman are unique and their nature is a unity. These are not about the dualistic composition of physical body and spiritual soul, but an entity in which the body finds expression in the whole. Stoll (1991, p. 6) demonstrates the spiritual nature of a person in this respect as, '... an animating, intangible principle that gives life to the physical organism...[it] integrates and transcends all other dimensions of a person... The literal breath of life'. Within the theological context spirituality is also about prayer, worship and a range of other practices that are associated with the development of spiritual life.

The well established holistic notion of a person being made up of the body, mind and spirit was shattered by Descartes (Bradshaw, 1994). Descartes' philosophy calls us to challenge the classical position on spirituality and offers an alternative. It proposed that an individual should be perceived as consisting of only reality, that is, mind. Everything else is secondary, and therefore more illusory in nature. Pietroni (1984) suggests that the overemphasis of physical patient care within medicine is due to Descartes' philosophy, which split off other aspects of the person and allowed them to become irrelevant. This was the inevitable outcome of Descartes' notion of the body as a machine. Descartes is blamed for the familiar medical view of a person as comprising of several systems. If one of these systems fails, it can be fixed irrespective of the individual's spiritual and psychological aspects.

We will return later to discuss the spiritual needs of clients who follow Christianity and Judaism. However, it is worth considering that some people in the West who do not claim to belong to any religious traditions may be described as humanists.

Humanists

It would be useful to note that a significant number of people in Western culture do not claim to adhere to religious beliefs. Between 25 to 30 per cent of people in Britain today do not have a religion (Narayanasamy, 1998). Some are simply silent on the issues of spirituality or claim to be humanists.

Eastern spirituality

In order to increase an awareness of the spiritual beliefs of some people which may be based on Eastern cultural traditions it would be useful to turn our attention to Eastern spirituality. When we refer to Eastern spirituality we are actually talking about spirituality that has its origins in Asia. It is well known that Asia, with its vast geographical expanse, has been a breeding ground for a rich cultural diversity in languages, customs, ethnic groupings, religious traditions and diverse economic levels. This rich mixture of cultural traditions has produced a variety of spiritual orientations or varieties of spiritualities. These being: **Asian Islamic** spirituality found in Pakistan, Afganistan, South East Asia and India; **Asian Buddhism** with different spiritual orientations are found in Theravada Thailand and Mahayana Japan; **Asian Christian** spirituality found in India that is contrastingly different from that of the Philippines where traces of Spanish influence are found.

There are great variations in the spiritual and intellectual life of Asians as well as similarities. The two great and most ancient civilisations of Asia, India and China, reflect sharp cultural contrasts. India lays its emphasis on the universals, underplays specific particulars and finds creativity in the act of negation. On the other hand, China is known for its concreteness, particulars and practicality. Such clear cultural variations will be evident in the spiritual orientation of some people who have their roots in any of these countries.

In spite of the differences, there is a common base of Asian spirituality. This becomes more apparent when it is contrasted with Western spirituality. Asian spirituality is concerned with un-differentiated totality before creation. Hence, the pantheistic view of all things being part of one creation, ie, God's creation. While, in Western spirituality a sharp distinction is drawn between the Creator God and His creations. The Western notion of dualism originates from the latter. In general, the fundamental contrast between Western and Asian spiritualities is that Asian spirituality is cosmological, while Western spirituality is eschatological (transcendent). Kosuke Koyama (1983) expresses this so eloquently:

> *While the cosmological spirituality proclaims that 'my help comes from heaven and earth', eschatological spirituality would say 'my help comes from the Lord who made heaven and earth'.*

p. 30

African spirituality

So far much focus in this chapter has been on Eastern spirituality (meaning Asian spirituality) but African spirituality needs some consideration. Africa, apart from its own cultural traditions, shows plurality in its spirituality. Like Asia, Africa is a vast continent with a diversity of culture and religions, contributed by native Africans, Africans of western and Arab origins, to name a few. In this respect Africa shows plurality when it comes to spirituality, and is predominantly influenced by Christianity and Islam. However, some people of African-Caribbean origins or traditions may express spiritual beliefs based on Rastafarianism which has its origins in Africa, Ethiopia, to be precise. It is strongest in Jamaica but has spread to other African-Caribbean communities, particularly in the USA and Europe. When Ras (Prince) Tafari was enthroned in Ethiopia in the 1930s as Emperor Haile Selassie, he was hailed as the black messiah who was predicted earlier to arrive in Africa.

Rastafarians accept some of the teachings of the Bible as it is the tradition of Ethiopia, basing their belief that God took human form, as Christ first, then as Ras Tafari. Rastafarians draw similarities with Israelites in that they liken the fate of all black people in the West to that of Israelites enslaved in Egypt and Babylon, and believe that they will not be free unless they return to Africa. This is interpreted by many Rastafarians as a spiritual state of mind rather than the actual place.

The ACCESS model

As a helpful strategy for the provision of sensitive care related to the cultural and spiritual needs of clients, the ACCESS model is suggested (Narayanasamy, 1999).

Assessment

A comprehensive assessment of the cultural aspects of a patient's lifestyle, health beliefs, and health practices will go a long way in enabling nurses to make decisions and judgements related to care interventions. The resulting care plans and interventions from this assessment should be considered in the light of the subsequent elements of the **ACCESS** model.

Transcultural care	
Assessment:	Focus on cultural aspect of client's lifestyle, health beliefs and health practices.
Communication:	Be aware of variations in verbal and non-verbal responses.
Cultural negotiation and compromise:	Become more aware of aspects of other people's culture as well as understanding of client's views and explain their problems.
Establishing respect and rapport:	A therapeutic relation which portrays genuine respect for clients' cultural beliefs and values is required.
Sensitivity:	Deliver diverse, culturally sensitive care to culturally diverse groups.
Safety	Enable clients to derive a sense of cultural safety.

Communication

The crux of transcultural care is communication. It is important for nurses to be aware that groups vary widely in their ideas about appropriate body stances and proximities, gestures, language, listening styles, and eye contact. For example, traditional Asians typically consider direct eye contact inappropriate and disrespectful. It is well known that language differences cause prolonged treatment as opposed to treatment for English-speaking patients (Sherer, 1993). Sometimes it may seem convenient to use a member of the patient's family as an interpreter to facilitate the communication process, but to save embarrassment in the presence of a family member, the patient may fabricate a new problem. Also, the interpreter may interpret rather than translate patient's problems. The nurse who is unfamiliar with the language may not realise whose views are being expressed.

Cultural negotiation and compromise

This requires that nurses make efforts to become more aware of aspects of other people's cultures, although it is almost impossible to be an expert in all cultures as there are more than 3000 cultures. Transcultural therapeutic interventions require cultural negotiation and compromise (Goode, 1993). This requires an understanding of how the patient views and explains the problem. It may include, for example, working in partnership with traditional healers like folk health practitioners or herbal therapists along with orthodox medical treatment. It may involve helping patients arrange traditional ceremonies connected with grieving and loss. In summary, nursing intervention should be orientated to patients' value position, showing sensitivity to the communication process and care expectations.

Establishing respect and rapport

Many of us can recall incidents when we were treated disrespectfully by other people. Disrespect evokes feelings of being devalued, leading to dents in our self-esteem. On the other hand, being respected produces a more positive effect in us. Nurses can establish respect and rapport as follows. The nurses can portray a genuine respect for the patient as a unique individual with needs which are influenced by cultural beliefs and values. This will enable clients to maintain their self-respect, leading to better self-esteem which is often at a low ebb during a health crisis. A positive nurse patient relationship is most likely to establish the rapport between them. This, in turn, will foster an atmosphere of trust in which a therapeutic relationship will be continued. All of these will lead to the development of mutual respect for each other's cultural beliefs and values.

Sensitivity

The primary concern of health care is to understand and deliver diverse, culturally sensitive care to diverse cultural groups. The care needs of the patients should be met through culturally adapted approaches. For nursing interventions to be effective, it is paramount that nurses show sensitivity to all aspects of patients' needs as well as the communication process involved. As part of this process, nurses require a knowledge of expected patient-specific patterns of communication. For example, it is important to recognise that certain terms, concepts and distinctions drawn in other languages are not easily translated into English. In such situations, patients whose first language is not English may sometimes draw from their indigenous vocabulary to make their points. Further understanding of the ways in which style and tone of communication may be used is required.

Safety

Patients need to derive a sense of cultural safety. Creating an environment where cultural adaptation takes place between nurses and patients promotes a sense of cultural safety. Patients who experience a sense of cultural safety are most likely to have trust in nurses and derive further benefits from the therapeutic relationship which is vital for interventions designed to meet cultural needs.

Conclusion

Spirituality and culture can be inextricably linked, each affecting the other. In many contexts spirituality could be the binding force that brings together cultures. The global impact of the spiritualities of certain religions have been significant and this is reflected in the population of many cities in the United Kingdom. Sensitivity to cultural and spiritual needs of patients from various cultural backgrounds is important and the **ACCESS** model can be useful in achieving this.

References

Bradshaw A (1994) *Lighting the Lamp: the Spiritual Dimensions of Nursing Care.* Scutari Press, London

Brown C (1993) Relating philosophy and theology. In: Keeley R (ed) *An Introduction to the Christian Faith.* Lynx Communication, Oxford

Goode EE (1993) The cultures of illness. *US News and World Report,* 15 Feb: 74–6

Koyama K (1983) No handle on the cross. Cited in: Wakefield CS (ed) (1989) *A Dictionary of Christian Spirituality.* SCM Press, London

Narayanasamy A (1999) Transcultural mental health nursing 2: Race, ethnicity and culture. *Br J Nurs* (14): 741–44

Narayanasamy A (1998) Religious and spiritual needs of older people. In: Pickering S, Thompson J (ed) (1988) *Promoting Positive Practice in Nursing Older People.* Baillière Tindal, London: 128–51

Pietroni P (1984) Holistic medicine: New map, old territory. *Br J Holistic Med* **1**(2): 3–13

Sherer, JL (1993) Crossing cultures: hospitals begin breaking down the barriers to care. *Hospitals* **20**: 29–31

Stoll RG (1991) The essence of spirituality. In: Carson VB (ed) *Spiritual Dimensions of Nursing Practice.* WB Saunders, London: 4–28

3

Spiritual needs

An holistic view is one that accepts that we all have needs which are social, psychological, physical and spiritual. Many of us have less trouble in identifying needs that are described as social, psychological and physical, but we struggle to identify spiritual needs. Although these needs are universal and can be applied to anyone, this chapter uses as a focus the meeting of spiritual needs for a Christian.

Spiritual needs

Bradshaw (1972) identified four types of needs. These are:

Normative needs: those identified by professional experts and reflect professional judgements and standards. Using the nursing process, nurses may assess patients' spiritual needs and use these data to develop spiritual care plans. Normative definitions of spiritual needs reflect professionals' views about the nature of health problems, which may vary from a lay person's perspective of their spiritual needs.

Comparative needs: assessing these usually entails estimation by professionals of which group of patients is in greater need of spiritual care. Assessing needs in this way may question how professionals judge which group needs what.

Felt needs: according to Bradshaw (1972), these are needs that individuals themselves identify. Patients may reveal these if asked appropriate questions related to their spiritual needs. However, sometimes individuals may feel unable to disclose felt needs or some may not believe themselves to be 'in need'.

Expressed needs: are what individuals say they need, it is usually the turning of a felt need into a request or call for attention.

However, Maslow (1968) postulated about a hierarchy of needs model in his humanistic theory of motivation. Maslow suggests that human needs can be placed along a hierarchy, where some will

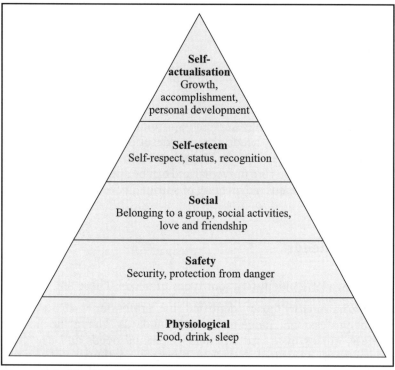

Figure 3.1: Maslow's hierarchy of needs

remain relatively unimportant until other needs have been fulfilled. The hierarchical nature of this model is well illustrated in *Figure 3.1*. Spiritual needs can be explained in terms of Maslow's hierarchy of needs. Apart from the basic physiological needs, humans use their senses to evoke certain feelings which are spiritual in nature, for example, feeling peaceful and happy. They can use their senses of hearing (eg. music) and smell (eg. aromatic) to induce a sense of spiritual uplift. Moving on to the next needs, safety needs – individuals need to feel secure and in this respect trusting relationships with others and their surroundings are considered to be spiritual needs (Narayanasamy, 1998). On attainment of these needs, individuals are driven to experience a sense of belonging and love needs. It is well documented in the literature that humans become dispirited if these needs are not met (Narayanasamy, 1998). As part of our spirituality we need to feel a sense of belonging and being loved. Next, our self-esteem needs are important to our spiritual well-being. We need to feel a sense of achievement, worthiness, approval and recognition.

Any barriers to the achievement of these needs may cause us much spiritual distress and these needs should be fulfilled before we move on to achieve self-actualisation, ie. self-fulfilment and realisation of our own potential. It can be postulated that complete spiritual well-being equates with achievement of all needs as given in Maslow's model of hierarchy of needs.

Although Maslow offers a convenient way of explaining spiritual needs, for two reasons his model can be problematic when applying it in practice. Firstly, needs placed in a hierarchy imply a degree of sophistication between needs in relative terms. In this respect some needs appear more important than others, and some at the top of the hierarchy can be perceived to be more unattainable than others. The portrayal of needs in an hierarchy may appear as a long struggle for some individuals to achieve self-actualisation. However, human experiences are not that clear-cut and cannot be easily explained in terms of a model such as the hierarchy of needs.

The second reason is that health care professionals experience difficulty in applying this model although it is popularly addressed in the literature. Factors such as stability, time, relationships, resources and so on act as barriers for professionals to promote spiritual well-being through conscious application of this model of needs. However, it offers a useful framework for understanding spirituality as a human dimension.

Case illustration

Mary, aged 78 years and widowed, lives alone and suffers from chronic arthritis. Her daughter and two sons visit her regularly and they are her constant source of support. Mary's arthritis gives her a lot of pain and sometimes she wonders why she has to suffer and tries to find meaning in her chronic disability. However, she finds meaning and hope through her prayers as she is a devoted Christian. Mary's daughter takes her to church whenever possible, where Mary finds the companionship of her fellow church-goers a good source of strength and support.

Her youngest son, John and his family have just returned to England after a long spell in Australia. He left England for Australia 20 years ago following an argument with his father. Mary feels guilty about the unresolved conflict between her son and husband and feels that reconciliation should have taken place before her husband's death. She tries to seek forgiveness for both through her prayers. Mary is delighted to see her grandchildren from Australia whom she had missed all these years and now finds inspiration and new meaning and hope in her life as a result of this. Mary's renewed hope has given her inspiration to rework her goals and she has found a new purpose in her life. Her arthritis is no longer the dominant feature in her life and she is able to resume painting and finds satisfaction in expressing creative talent through her artistic work.

Activity

Identify Mary's spiritual needs and list them below.

Feedback on activity

We express our spiritual needs in a variety of ways and forms. Your list of Mary's spiritual needs may include the following:

* the need for meaning and purpose
* the need for love and harmonious relationships
* the need for forgiveness
* the need for a source of hope and strength
* the need for trust
* the need for expression of personal beliefs and values
* the need for spiritual practices, expression of concept of God or Deity and creativity.

Meaning and purpose

Many people tend to find themselves wrestling with the meaning and purpose in life during a crisis, whether in health or illness. In the earlier case illustration Mary tried to find meaning in her suffering. 'Meaning' in this context can be defined as the reason given to a particular life experience by the individual. The search for meaning is a primary force in life. This drives us to search for meaning to life in general and discovering meaning in suffering in particular. We need to make sense out of our life and illness. Mary, in the case illustration above, found new meaning and purpose in her changed circumstances.

There is evidence to suggest that patients struggle with finding a source of meaning and purpose in their lives (Peterson and Nelson, 1987; Burnard, 1990). It is suggested that people with a sense of meaning and purpose survive more readily in very difficult circumstances, including illness and suffering. There is some truth in the expression that he who has a 'why' to life can bear with almost any 'how'.

Many of us approach the task of life in a variety of ways and so our ability to cope with a crisis varies. We can find meaning and purpose in the experience of suffering. There is a distinction between the religious and the apparently non-religious person in the way that they approach spirituality, that is, the religious person experiences his existence not merely as a task but as a mission, and is aware of his taskmaster, the source of his mission. That source is God.

In a crisis, such as bereavement, the person experiences meaninglessness, that is, the person expresses a sense of bewilderment and loss of meaning. For example, the person with a diagnosis of HIV infection, the survivor of a traumatic road accident, the family of a child who dies, the patient in a mental health unit, all cry out for help in search of meaning and desperately seek to talk to someone who will give attention and time to their exploration of meaning and purpose. The nurse is very often the nearest person to whom sufferers can reach out.

In a person searching for meaning and purpose there may be a need for exploration of spiritual issues. In some instances the person in search of spirituality may want to talk about religious feelings or lack of them. The person may not be asking advice or opinions but just for an opportunity to talk about feelings, to express doubts and anguish. Such opportunity for expression can bring about clarity and a renewed sense of meaning and purpose.

A person who has a strong religious conviction and senses God, still needs encouragement to adapt to unexpected changes. He is likely to experience hope even when his usual support systems let him down. His experience of God reassures him that God will never fail him. The nurse may have to act as a catalyst in providing the opportunity for finding meaning and purpose in a crisis by establishing his relationship with God.

Love and harmonious relationships

Our need for love and harmonious relationships goes hand in hand with a need for meaning and purpose. The need for love and to give love are fundamental human needs (Maslow, 1968) which last throughout life from childhood to old age. A spiritually distressed person requires unconditional love, that is love that has no strings attached to it. This is sometimes referred to as 'in spite of' love. The spiritually distressed person does not have to earn it by being good or attractive or wealthy. The person is simply loved for the way he or she is, regardless of faults or ignorance or bad habits or deeds. Mary, our lady in the illustration above, met her spiritual need in this area from her family and fellow church-goers.

The manifestations of the need for love are self-pity, depression, insecurity, isolation, and fear. These are indicators of a need for love from oneself, other people and God, if the person is religious. The person receiving this kind of love experiences feelings of self-worth, joy, security, belonging, hope and courage.

The following can be identified as signs of spiritual problems in a person who may need to receive love to resolve some of them:

* worries and expressions of concerns about how the rest of the family will manage after his or her death
* expression of feelings of a loss of faith in God
* reluctance to discuss feelings about dying with close friends and family
* failure to call on others for help when needed
* expression of fear of tests and diagnosis (a universal fear)
* expression of feeling lack of support from others
* behaviour that reflects he/she 'should' be conforming to the behaviour of a 'good' patient or person
* refusal to co-operate with health care regime
* expression of guilt feelings
* thoughts of confession and feelings about shameful events
* expression of anger with self/others
* expressions of ambivalent feelings toward God
* expression of despondency during illness/hospitalisation
* expression of resentment toward God
* expression of loss of self-value due to decreasing physical capacity
* expression of fear of God's anger
* desperate 'clinging' to those who talk to them.

The spiritually distressed person also has a need to give love, which may include, for example, worries about financial status of family during hospitalisation/separation from family and worries about separation from others during death.

Forgiveness

Forgiveness can be seen from two sides: the need to both give and receive. We saw in Mary's case the need for forgiveness and this is one of the principal causes of spiritual distress. A person who experiences spiritual distress expresses feelings of guilt and requires the opportunity for forgiveness. Mary sought forgiveness for her son and husband through her prayers. Guilt often emerges when a person experiences the realisation that s/he has failed to live up to his/her own expectations or the expectations of others. For example, we may first experience guilt as a child when our behaviour does not measure up to the standards set for us by our parents. We contradict them and do the very things we are told not to do. Guilt breeds in us in the form of regrets not only for the things we have done but also for what we have not done. Unresolved conflicts in relationships can result in feelings of guilt.

The feelings of guilt may be expressed as feelings of paranoia, hostility, worthlessness, defensiveness, withdrawal, psychosomatic complaints, rationalisations, criticism of self, others and God and 'scapegoating'. Forgiveness may bring a feeling of joy, peace and elation, and a sense of renewed self-worth. Confession of sin is one way in which some people achieve forgiveness from God.

Hope and strength

Hope is seen by psychologists and sociologists as necessary for life and without it we begin to die (Simsen, 1988). For many of us our sense of hope can be a powerful motivator in enabling an open attitude toward new ways of coping. Mary, in the case illustration, achieves new hope and strength from reconciliation with her son and his family. The spiritually distressed person may experience a feeling of hopelessness. The hopeless person may see no way out; there may be no other possibilities other than those dreaded.

We met in Mary's situation her new goals and a renewed purpose as a result of her son's arrival from Australia. We thrive on good relationships with others and this is another facet of our hope. This includes relationships with others, ourselves and the world, what a person believes and what is desired is possible. According to Soeken and Carson (1987):

> *Ultimate hope resides in God and belief that the Supreme Being will impart meaning to individual lives and sufferings. Both components of hope are important for the patient with chronic illness.*

p. 610

Hope is also necessary for future plans. Further sources of our hope include seeking support, love and the stability provided by important relationships in our life, and putting into action future plans. Mary successfully achieves all of these through her loved ones and friends in the case illustration in this chapter. If the patient believes in God, then hope in God is important. This hoping in God is the ultimate source of strength and supersedes all aspirations that are transitional.

Hope is closely related to our need for a source of strength. A source of hope provides the strength that we may need. A source of strength gives us the courage needed to face innumerable odds in a crisis. The main source of hope and strength is found by individuals who pray because of their faith in God/Supreme Being. Haase's (1987) study found that the subjects concurred that belief in the power of prayer helped them cope with medical procedures and opportunities to express their faith helped them to resolve the situation they described. For some, communication with God and prayer is a source of strength. More recent studies suggest similar findings (Narayanasamy, 1995; Benson and Stark, 1996). For most of us a message of hope provides new energy, strength, and courage to preserve or revise goals or plan and these were apparent in Mary's situation.

Trust

We feel secure when we can establish a trusting relationship with others. The spiritually distressed person needs an environment that conveys a trusting relationship. Such an environment is one which demonstrates that carers make themselves accessible to others, both physically and emotionally. Trusting is the ability to place confidence in the trustworthiness of others, which is essential for spiritual health and total well-being. Learning to trust in an environment which is alien can be a daunting task and not an easy skill to accomplish.

Personal beliefs and values

The opportunity to express personal values and beliefs is a known spiritual need (Narayanasamy, 2000). In this sense spirituality refers to anything that a person considers to be of highest value in life. Mary shares her beliefs with her companions at the church and expresses these through her prayers. Her spiritual needs are easily met because she has the opportunity through the support of her family. Personal values which may be highly regarded by an individual include, for example, beliefs of a formalised religious path, whereas for others it may be, for example, a set of very personal philosophical statements, or perhaps a physical activity.

Spiritual practices, concept of god/deity, and creativity

The opportunity to express our needs related to spiritual practices, the concept of God or Deity and creativity may present as a feature of spirituality. The concept of God or Deity may be an important function in the inner life of a person. The need to carry out spiritual practices concerning God or Deity may be too daunting for the person if the opportunity is not available or the environment is alien or unreceptive to this need.

Our creative needs may feature in spirituality. Mary achieves spirituality as a creative need through her paintings. A religious minister in Connecticut Hospice uses the arts as an avenue to the spirit in which actors, writers, musicians, and artists of a university are invited to exhibit their work and give performances (Wald, 1989).

Human development and spiritual needs

Certain spiritual needs tend to feature during our personal development and growth. During infancy, trust is a major spiritual need and during our childhood we learn to understand concepts about religion from our parents and people close to us. In adolescence we tend to search for meaning and value in life. For example, fears can be regarded as clues to children's spiritual needs and such fears may include the dark, sudden movements, loud noises, loss of support, pain, fear of strangers or strange objects, heights, or anticipated unpleasant situations. Unmet needs for love and loving relationships may be manifest as those fears. So, meeting the infant's need for basic trust has an impact on the long-term spiritual development of that individual.

During childhood, we learn to understand religious concepts from parents and other people in our environment. The child's inquisitive mind may prompt him to ask questions about basic issues of life, for example: 'What is God?' 'Why doesn't John have a Christmas Tree?' and 'How come Granny went to heaven?' The spiritual needs of the child include a need for love and security. Also, the child is likely to imitate his parent's faith, however, some of his concept of faith may be based on fantasy. The child also learns to recognise what is 'good' or 'bad' from his parents and significant others. During crises, such as admission to hospital, the child often has great difficulty with verbal expression of his spiritual concerns. The death of a loved one may make this even more of a problem. The child does not understand that death is universal, inevitable and irreversible.

In adolescence the search for meaning and value in life may feature as a spiritual need. Problems arise as a result of conflicts within the family because of moral standards set by parents. Conflicts may arise as a result of double standards expected from parents. Because of these conflicts the adolescent's source of strength and support could come from peer group.

During young adulthood searching takes place for trust, for love, for hope, and forgiveness. There may be an experience of tension, expectations and spiritual struggle. It is also a time for re-structuring religious, moral and ethical values. During the stage of young adulthood there may be a period in which re-orientation and growth in the spiritual realm takes place.

In middle years, the questioning of life precipitated by the death of parents or peers, children leaving home, plans for retirement, or an awareness of our physical failings may feature. The four common spiritual needs in middle age are:

1. The need for meaning and purpose in life.
2. The need to be forgiven.
3. The need to receive love.
4. The need for hope and creativity.

In old age, a stock of life's successes and failures is often taken together with a renewal of religious faith and spiritual beliefs. Many people experience a more positive self-concept as a result of accomplishment and worth. Some may find great social and spiritual fulfilment in having some kind of religious affiliation. Religious ceremonies such as marriages, baptisms, and burials may become significant. Religious expression may be fulfilled by attendance at the church or place of worship. Church or religious affiliation promotes feelings of hope and purpose to life for many older people.

Summary

In this chapter an attempt has been made to identify spiritual needs. These include the need for meaning and purpose; the need for love and harmonious relationships; the need for forgiveness; the need for a source of hope and strength; the need for trust; the need for expression of personal beliefs and values; and the need for spiritual practice, expression of concept of God or Deity and creativity. These are by no means exclusive, but commonly recognised as within the province of nursing to incorporate into care plans as part of spiritual care of patients. Finally, certain spiritual needs as a feature of our development were outlined.

References

Benson H, Stark M (1996) *Timeless Healing. The power of biology of belief.* Simon & Schuster, London

Bradshaw J (1972) The concept of social need. *New Society* **19**(3): 640–3

Burnard P (1990) Learning to care for the spirit. *Nurs Standard* **14**(18): 38–39

Haase JE (1987) Components of Courage in Chronically Ill Adolescents: A phenomenological Study. *Adv Nurs Science* **9**: 64

Maslow AR (1968) *Toward a Psychology of Being.* Van Nostrand, New York

Narayanasamy A (2000) Spiritual care and mental health competence. In: Thompson T, Mathias P (eds) *Lyttle's Mental Health and Disorder.* Baillière Tindall, London: 305–324

Narayanasamy A (1998) Religious and spiritual needs of older people. In: Pickering A, Thompson J (eds) *Promoting Positive Practice in Nursing Older People*. Baillière Tindall, London: 128–151

Narayanasamy A (1995) Spiritual care of chronically ill patients. *J Clin Nurs* **4**: 397–400

Peterson E, Nelson K (1987) How to meet your clients' spiritual needs. *J Psychosoc Nurs* **25**(5): 34–38

Simsen B (1988) Nursing the spirit. *Nurs Times* **1**(84): 37, 31–35

Soeken KL, Carson YJ (1987) Responding to the spiritual needs of the chronically ill? *Nurs Clin North Am* **22**(3): 603–611

Wald FS (1989) The widening scope of spiritual care. *Am J Hospice Care* July/August: 40–43

Annodated bibliography

Biddulph S, Biddulph S (1999) *Love, Laughter and Parenting.* Dorling Kindersley, London

Readers wishing more information on the practicalities of dealing with children's spirituality may find this book useful. It is aimed at parents but health carers can pick up useful hints. The book offers the following tips: teaching children to respect other's feelings and to show gentleness towards insects, animals etc; enjoying the beauty of nature and environment; developing positive attitudes to themselves and others, including teaching them that there is some good in everyone and that things have a way of resolving; encouraging children to value diversity and respect differences with regard to people of different ages, disabilities, ethnicity, cultures and talents; never to put down other groups, religions or races in front of children; explaining in plain language questions children may ask about spirituality.

4

Religious/spiritual beliefs and needs

As we have seen earlier, spirituality and religion are inextricably connected and sometimes it is difficult to separate the two. In order to provide satisfactory spiritual care we have to understand the religious needs of patients who have strong religious faiths. In many hospitals, particularly in inner cities, nursing involves caring for patients from a variety of religious and cultural backgrounds. An understanding of these differing religious needs is an important prerequisite for spiritual care (Murray and Zentner, 1989). This chapter introduces the major religions of the world. These include: Christianity, Islam, Hinduism, and Judaism. Specific religious needs, related life events and activities of living are outlined in each of the sections on religion. The chapter also addresses the beliefs and practices of Pagans and Humanists. Please note it is beyond the scope of this book to provide a wider coverage that all religions rightly deserve. Only the bare essentials have been possible to cover. Every attempt has been made to ensure that accuracy is reflected, however, apologies are given in advance for any omissions or errors related to any of the faith/beliefs addressed in this book.

Buddhism

Buddhism was founded in India by Gautama Siddhartha (Buddha, meaning 'the enlightened') who lived from c.563–c.583 BC. Buddhism embraces the following: Four Noble Truths and the Noble Eightfold Path. The four Noble Truths are:

1. Suffering is universal.
2. The cause of suffering is craving, or selfish desire.
3. The use of suffering is the elimination of craving.
4. The way to eliminate craving is to follow the middle way, a technique that embodies the Noble Eightfold Path.

The Path consists of:

1.	Right knowledge.	5.	Right means of livelihood.
2.	Right intention.	6.	Right effort.
3.	Right speech.	7.	Right mindfulness.
4.	Right conduct.	8.	Right concentrations.

Buddhism, more of a philosophy than a religion, enables its follower to strive to achieve an impersonal ultimate reality through a purifying life of ethical thinking and by carrying out good deeds. The ultimate goal of a Buddhist is the achievement of Nirvana – a state of liberation, ie. freeing one from suffering, death and rebirth and all otherworldly bonds. Nirvana is the highest transcendent consciousness.

Buddhists believe in reincarnation, but they do not accept the Hindus' view of the transmigration of souls through various forms of life. For some Buddhists, monastic life is important, in which withdrawal from the mainstream of life and relinquishing the eating of meat and owning of personal property is possible. Many Buddhists, in their early years, spend a part of their lives as monks, but most return to mainstream life. Essentially, most Buddhists are compassionate, avoid killing animals, and may be vegetarians.

Many regard Buddhism as the gentlest of religions. It has spread to all continents and its dominating influence is found in Japan, Manchuria, Mongolia, China, Tibet, Burma, Thailand, Cambodia and Sri Lanka. Buddhism has encouraged humanity in the form of tolerance, non-violence, respect for the individual, love of nature, and the spiritual equality of human beings. There is a variation in the way the religion is understood and practised among Buddhists.

Main points affecting nursing care

Diet

⌘ Many Buddhists are vegetarian as all killing is forbidden.

Dying

⌘ The most important consideration is the state of mind. Provision of peace and quiet in which to meditate is vital. Buddhists may wish to chant in order to reach a desired state of peace.

⌘ No special requirements after death although a monk of the patient's school should be contacted as soon as possible.

Christianity

Christianity in some form will probably be the religion with which many nurses and students of nursing who read this book are familiar. Christianity is the religion that is based on Jesus Christ. It is the largest and most universal religion of more than one billion believers. Beliefs of Christianity are explained within the Old and the New Testament books of the Holy Scriptures (the Bible). Those who follow Christianity believe that God became man in the form of Jesus Christ, that he was crucified, rose again and ascended to heaven. Christians are usually baptised, many as babies, and this marks their entry into the Christian faith.

There are seven sacraments including baptism and the Eucharist. The Eucharist/Holy Communion/Mass is the principal sacrament. This involves the distribution among church members of blessed bread and wine, symbolising the body and blood of Jesus. It is important to identify to which church/denomination a patient belongs.

The three main groups of Christians in the United Kingdom are:

Anglicans (Church of England, Church of Ireland, Church in Wales and the Scottish Episcopal Church).

Roman Catholics.

Free Church (including Methodist, Baptist, Presbyterian, Salvation Army, United Reformed Church, Church of Scotland, Quaker, The Lutheran Church. Pentecostal/Elim and independent churches such as Bethesda Emmanuel).

Within the hospital there are chaplains to offer ministry to these groups, and they can be contacted via hospital chaplaincy/ Department of Spiritual and Pastoral Care.

Anglicanism

Names

⌘ Christians have two or three names: christian name; middle name; surname – their family name.

Main points affecting nursing care

Food

⌘ While there are no particular dietary needs, some may not wish to eat meat on Friday, and may eat fish instead.

Fasting

⌘ Some may wish to fast prior to receiving Holy Communion.

Blood transfusions/transplants

⌘ There are no religious objections to these.

Prayer worship

⌘ Sunday is the main day for religious celebration, although prayer may be practised at any time. It is important that if a patient is unable to get to the chapel for quiet prayer, every effort should be made to provide an area within the ward for that time.

⌘ Easter and Christmas are the main celebrations.

Birth

⌘ There are no specific rites associated with birth. Should a child be ill at birth or shortly after, baptism should be offered to the parents and the chaplain called. If there is no time to call the chaplain, any member of staff is able to baptise. This is performed by pouring a little water over the child's forehead, while saying '(**name of child**), I baptise you in the name of the Father and of the Son and of the Holy Spirit, Amen.'

⌘ If a child dies without baptism being offered, some may feel that the child has been excluded from God's family.

Death and dying

⌘ There is belief in life after death and as death approaches some may wish to have prayers said, or for anointing to take place. The chaplains are available for this. They are also available to talk with the family.

⌘ Last offices can be carried out by staff or family, as is appropriate.

⌘ There is no religious objection to post-mortem.

Roman Catholicism

Names

⌘ Roman Catholics tend to have four names: christian name – their first name; second name; confirmation name – traditionally the name of a saint; surname – their family name.

Main points affecting nursing care

Food

⌘ Friday is traditionally a day to refrain from eating meat, but this is not compulsory.

Fasting

⌘ While the sick are not expected to fast, some Catholics will fast during Lent. Fasting and abstinence, ie. from meat, is compulsory on Ash Wednesday and Good Friday.

Blood transfusions/transplants

⌘ There are no religious objections to these.

Prayer/worship

⌘ Sunday remains the main day for worship, with Easter and Christmas being the main celebrations. It is usual for a priest to hear a person's confession and it may be necessary to find a quiet area within the ward for this.
⌘ As with Anglicans a quiet area for prayer may be required.

Birth

⌘ As with the Anglicans there are no specific rites associated with birth, however should a baby be ill, it is important to offer baptism. Should a priest be unable to attend, a member of staff could carry out the baptism.

Death and dying

⌘ Roman Catholics believe in life after death. When a person is ill, they can receive the Sacrament of the Sick. This is adapted, depending on the severity of the illness and can be given again if the patient's condition changes. This sacrament is to symbolise forgiveness, healing and reconciliation. This is usually preferred when a person is seriously ill.

⌘ A small bottle of **holy water** may be placed near the bed, **this should not be removed**.

⌘ If a priest is with the patient at the point of death or soon after, they can administer the last rites. The main reason to call a priest out after death is for them to be with the relatives, therefore it may not be necessary to call them out if there are no relatives present and the patient has died. The wishes of the patient and family regarding the last rites should be honoured.

⌘ Last offices can be carried out by the nursing staff or family as appropriate. There is no religious objection to post-mortem.

⌘ Burial is preferred but cremation is permitted.

Free Church

This group covers a large number of churches, who all have their own traditions and ways of interpreting the Bible. They are very similar to the Anglicans and only any differences will be listed.

Main points affecting nursing care

Birth

⌘ There are no rites associated with the birth of a child. As with Anglicans, if a child/baby is seriously ill they can be baptised in hospital. Should there not be time to call a chaplain, a member of staff can carry this out as with the Anglicans.

⌘ The Society of Friends and the Salvation Army do not baptise, and the Baptists are usually baptised in adulthood using full immersion in water.

Death and dying

⌘ Free Church patients believe in life after death. They are usually happy to see any Free Church minister, not necessarily their own.

⌘ Some Free Church patients may wish for prayers and anointing.

⌘ Prayers may be said at the bedside at the point of death or just afterwards, and they may also be said in the viewing room.

⌘ Both burial and cremation are acceptable.

Hinduism

People of Indian origin or ancestry are likely to be Hindus although some may follow other faiths. Approximately 360,000 of the world's 700 million Hindus live in Britain. Many of the British Hindu families have not migrated directly from India, but from East Africa or, in some cases, from other parts of the world including Trinidad and Fiji.

It is estimated that about 70 per cent of Britain's Hindu community originate from the western Indian state of Gujarat. Their customs, their dialect, as well as their food, their festivals and styles of worship, reflect this. Cultural variations in religious practices among Hindus are common. These differ according to their ancestral region, their caste (social grouping) and the gurus (or spiritual teachers) whose path they follow.

The second-largest group of Britain's Hindus, an estimated 15 per cent, have their roots in Punjab, a state divided between India and Pakistan in 1947. There are also smaller Hindu communities in Britain which originate from other Indian states such as West Bengal, Maharashtra and Tamil Nadu.

Hindus believe in one God. God, however, can be worshipped in many forms; the important ones being Brahma (the Creator), Vishnu (the Preserver), and Shiva (the Destroyer). Hindus hold beliefs about non-violence and reincarnation.

Reincarnation is the cycle of birth and re-birth (Hinduism also believes in transmigration of souls). It is based on the notion that individuals are responsible for their actions in each life, and undergo a cycle of rebirth until their lifestyles raise above their previous lives and unite them with God. Current lifestyles of Hindus are pre-destined according to the behaviour in the last life.

Religion is a way of life for many Hindus and one that is constant and pervades all aspects of their lives. The Hindu sacred book is the *Bhagavad-Gita*. The *Ramayana* and *Mahabhrata* are the two great epics in Hinduism. In recent years the latter was shown as a long television series in Britain.

Many Hindus worship at shrines in their homes, in front of various pictures of incarnations of the Deities, and burn incense. There is no standard form of worship in Hinduism. Some Hindus meditate, some pray, some combine meditation, prayer and physical exercises as in Hatha-yoga.

Temples have sprung up in many places as far apart as Glasgow and Southampton. More recently, the new Hindu temple in London received much media publicity for its Deity's miraculous abilities to drink milk when fed with a spoon. Some other places of worship for Hindus are the Swaminarayan temples in Bolton, Leicester and London, or Bhativedanta Manor in Letchmore Heath, Hertfordshire. At these temples, devotees express beliefs led by gurus within the Hindu family of traditions. One other centre of worship in Highgate, London, the Lord Murugan Temple, reflects linguistic and cultural identity, in this case, the language and traditions of the south Indian state of Tamil Nadu.

Important festivals

Holi (end of March): This is a spring festival of Krishna, representing the gaiety and fun of Krishna in his youth. It is common for Hindu children to throw coloured powder and water at each other.

New Year (mid April).

Diwali (mid October): The festival of lights.

Raksha Bandhan (August): This festival is also called *Rakhi*. A sister ties a multicoloured thread around her brother's wrist. It signifies the bond of mutual love and trust between brothers and sisters. Sometimes a woman who does not have a brother ties the Rakhi on the cousins or any other male relative. In this way, he becomes the so-called 'brother' and then it is his duty to protect his 'sister' from troubles and dangers. This tradition promotes the message of universal brotherhood.

Main points affecting nursing care

Prayer

❖ Many Hindus pray at least once a day, at sunrise. They may wish to wash and change their clothes prior to prayer.

Privacy/hygiene

⌘ Hindu women dress modestly and may wish to be seen by a female doctor if possible and be attended to by female nurses.

⌘ Should the spouse be present, some Hindus will find it hard to discuss issues surrounding pain, genito-urinary or bowel matters.

⌘ Water will be required for washing after use of bedpan.

⌘ Hindus will probably require water for ritual hand washing and mouth rinsing before and after meals.

Birth

⌘ The older relative may require the mother of a new-born baby to rest for 40 days.

Abortion/family planning

⌘ Hindu women feel that they have a duty to produce a son. Needs of the family are more important than those of society. May be against abortion.

Transfusion

⌘ Generally accepted.

Diet

⌘ Killing any living soul for consumption is considered a sin.

⌘ The cow is a sacred animal and is never eaten. Many are vegetarians. They may refuse to eat off plates that have had meat on them.

⌘ Some Hindus may eat chicken, eggs or onions although this is cultural and not for religious reasons.

Dying

⌘ Devout Hindus will derive comfort from readings from the Hindu scriptures. Some may wish to lie on the floor to be close to Mother Earth, or to release a bed for someone else. The family may bring items for the dying patient to touch prior to donation to the needy. Devout Hindus will probably wish to die at home which has great religious and social significance.

⌘ Hindu priests may be needed to perform certain rituals and blessings. Nursing staff can wash the body. Religious objects must not be removed.

⌘ Adults are cremated ideally within 24 hours of death. The eldest son is responsible for funeral arrangements. (If there is no son, then a male relative will take responsibility.)

⌘ Post-mortems are disliked, but there is no religious prohibition.

Other considerations

⌘ The Hindu faith is centred on the transmigration of the soul with indefinite reincarnation. As a soul moves from body to body it hopes to become purer and purer until it reaches God.

Islam

Muslims are followers of Islam and two million of them live in Britain. Most Muslims are born in the UK, but their families may have come from Turkey, Somalia, West Africa, South Asia (mainly, Pakistan, Bangladesh and India). In the UK most people are of Pakistani or Bangladeshi origin, and some with Indian ancestry are Muslims. Some British people have converted to the Muslim faith (Narayanasamy and Andrews, 2000).

More than a fifth of the world's population practice Islam. There are Muslim communities in more than 120 countries, the largest being in Indonesia.

Islam originated in the Middle East at the beginning of the seventh century by Prophet Muhammad. It is the youngest of the major world religions (Narayanasamy and Andrews, 2000). Muslims believe in one God, 'Allah', and Muhammad, his prophet, provides the key to Muslim beliefs. Islam means 'peaceful submission to Allah's will'. The beliefs and way of life of Muslims, Islam, is laid down in the Qur'an (Koran) as well as the life and teaching of the Prophet Muhammad.

There is a great deal of similarity in the practices and beliefs of all Muslims, however, some differences exist in the interpretations and explanation of the Qur'an by the main (two) sects in Islam – the Sunni and Shi'ah believers (McAvoy and Donaldson, 1990). Sunni Muslims adhere to the traditions of the early elected 'Khalifahs', or leaders, who were obedient to the example and teaching of Muhammad. Shi'ah Muslims also follow the descendants of Muhammad, with extra beliefs and customs. Large numbers of Shi'ahs are found in Iran and Iraq. In Britain and the rest of the world, most Muslims are Sunni.

According to history, the earliest Muslim communities in Britain were composed of former seamen who had settled near the docklands of Cardiff, Liverpool and South Shields. During the labour shortage of the boom years of the 1960s in Britain, the Government's recruitment of overseas labour brought many people from India and Pakistan to the Midlands and the North. Recently, Muslims have come from Bangladesh, mainly to east London. Bangladesh, formerly East Pakistan, became independent in 1971.

Five Pillars

To Muslims, the five central or pillars of belief are important. These show them how their beliefs should be put into action in daily life.

1. *The Shahadah* is the declaration of one's faith, which is repeated several times a day: 'There is no God but Allah, and Muhammad is His Messenger'.
2. *Salah* is the formal prayer, recited five times daily, at home, in the mosque or at the place of work. This daily prayer is carried out in Arabic at dawn, noon, mid-afternoon, just after sunset and after dark. The prayers may be recited in any clean place and extra prayers may be observed at any time. Muslims carry out ritualistic washing and take off their shoes before prayer, for cleanliness.
3. *Sawm*. Muslims should fast during the daylight hours in the month of Ramadan, health permitting. Fasting focuses the minds of Muslims to be conscious of Allah and reminds them of the poor and hungry. It brings them to the same level as the poor, thus fostering the notion of equality. Ramadan is the time for intense studying of the Qur'an and for practising self-discipline and charity.
4. *Zakat*. Muslims who can afford it are obliged to give at least 2.5 per cent of their untouched wealth annually for the welfare of the community, ie. to support the mosque, charities and others in need.
5. *Hajj*. The pilgrimage to Mecca should be made once in a lifetime, if possible, to visit the Ka'bah.

Many Muslims visit the mosque, an important feature of their lives. It is a place for individual and communal prayer as well as a facility for study and the discussion of community matters. On Fridays, many Muslims attend the congregational prayer (*jum'ah*) at midday.

Muslim dress

Modesty in dressing is expected of men and women. Women normally cover their head, arms and legs. Some Muslim women may observe strict dress code, that is, cover their faces too when outside the home. Of course, dress rules are interpreted differently in different places and by different people.

Muslim diet

In Islam all meat must be *halal* (permitted), which means the animal has to have been killed and blessed in a certain way. Pork and pork-based products are forbidden because Muslims believe these are unclean.

Alcohol is strictly forbidden as well because it clouds people's minds and leads them to forget their duties to Allah, such as prayer.

Main points affecting nursing care

Prayer

- This takes place on 'clean' ground (eg. a prayer mat), facing Mecca, without shoes and with the head covered. Muslims will require access to running water to complete their ritual wash (*Wudu*) before prayer.
- Prayer occurs: after dawn; at noon; mid afternoon; after sunset; at night.

Birth

- A prayer is whispered in the baby's ear.
- Staff should refrain, if possible, from shaving the new-born's hair. Parents will do this in order to weigh the hair so that an equivalent weight in gold can be given to charity.

Hygiene

- Access to running water will be required after use of a bedpan in order to perform ritual cleansing. If the genital area is not cleaned with running water, the Muslim patient may feel 'unclean' and therefore unable to pray.
- Hands, feet, face and mouth will be washed before prayer.

⌘ Women are required to wash the whole body after menstruation. Fresh running water is required, so showers are preferred to baths.

Privacy

⌘ Muslim women are not usually allowed to be examined by male doctors or attended by male nursing staff. Free mixing of sexes is prohibited so a mixed sex ward would be inappropriate. Women may wish to keep their heads and bodies covered at all times.

Peace and Blessing Be Upon Him

⌘ This is used after every mention of the Prophet Muhammad.

Fasting

⌘ During Ramadan, the Muslims may take nothing into the body by mouth, nose, injection or suppository between dawn and sunset.
⌘ The very ill are excused from this but may not wish to be.

Diet

⌘ Only *halal* meat may be eaten (this is slaughtered according to prayer and ritual). Pork, carrion and blood are forbidden as are products made from, or cooked, in them.

Dying

⌘ The family may sit with the dying patient and recite verses from the Qur'an. A special prayer (*Shahadah*) may be whispered to the patient who may wish to face Mecca as they die (eg. facing south-east for those in Britain).

Post-mortems

⌘ These are disliked because the body belongs to God and should not be cut out, harmed or donated.

Procedure to be followed in the event of the death of a Muslim patient

⌘ The eyes may be closed.
⌘ The mouth may be closed by use of a bandage.
⌘ The body should be straightened by first flexing the elbows, shoulders, knees and hips before straightening. This is thought to delay stiffening, making laying out easier later.

⌘ The head should be turned towards the right shoulder to enable burial facing Mecca.

⌘ Hair and nails must not be trimmed.

⌘ Do not wash the body.

⌘ Cover with a plain white sheet with no religious emblems.

⌘ Do not remove any thread or religious symbols from the neck or wrists.

Judaism

Judaism is the faith of the Jewish people, numbering around 300,000 followers in Britain. Actual numbers are difficult to gauge, as there is a lack of consensus about how to determine 'who is a Jew'. Traditionally, whoever is born to a Jewish mother is considered be a Jew. However, there are also thousands of 'secular' Jews who show no affiliation towards the religion in any outward form.

In modern Judaism there are three main divisions: Orthodox, Conservative and Reform. Reform Judaism is somewhat more liberal than the other two divisions in its beliefs and practices. Orthodox Judaism is the stricter of the two, and adherents hold the beliefs that God gave the law and that this should be followed precisely as written. Certain beliefs are shared by all Jews:

* God is the one and only God
* he is holy and sacred
* by his word he creates, rules, and judges the world and people
* he will bring history to fulfilment in the messianic age.

The theory and practice of Jewish ethics include:

❖ The moral law comes from God and, as such it is absolute, universal, revealed, and human.

❖ The law consists of commandments of God which are interpreted by the Rabbi, to be studied and followed by all, as a blessing for them and for the world.

Synagogues are Jewish centres of worship, education and socialising. Worship in the synagogue takes the form of prayers and readings, especially from the Torah. The Torah contains five books of the Bible and is considered to be the most important of Jewish sacred writings. The worship is often led by a rabbi or a singing leader called a 'cantor'.

The Jewish home is valued as more important than the synagogue for ensuring the continuing of the Jewish faith. Followers of this faith eat only food that has been prepared in accordance with God's law to make it *kosher* (fit). Meat and milk products must never be eaten at the same time or prepared with the same utensils and many foods, including pork and shellfish, are forbidden by the Torah.

The Sabbath

Sabbath (*Shabbat* in Hebrew) is the Jewish holy day, which begins at sunset on Friday and lasts until nightfall on Saturday. It is a day for rest and contemplation.

Festivals

Rosh Hashanah is a festival for the Jewish New Year which falls in September or October.

Yom Kippur or the Day of Atonement (making amends) comes ten days after Jewish New Year. This is the most sacred day in the Jewish year and is spent in prayer, fasting and asking God's forgiveness for wrongdoing.

Passover or Pessa, falls in March or April, signifies the night when the Israelite children were saved or 'passed over' by the plague before their escape from slavery in Egypt.

Seder is the most important ceremony. It is a meal in which some of the food and drink has a special meaning.

At ***Hanukkah***, the festival of lights which falls in November or December, a candlestick with nine branches is used.

Main points affecting nursing care

Prayer

⌘ Male patients may wear their skull caps and require privacy at the following times:

* before breakfast – this may take half an hour and require the wearing of a prayer shawl and plylacteries (leather boxes containing passages from the Bible bound around the head and hand)
* afternoon prayer – may only take five minutes
* evening prayer – may only take five minutes.

Privacy/hygiene

⌘ Orthodox women will wish to keep their body, hair and limbs covered at all times.

Diet

⌘ Orthodox Jews adhere to a kosher diet. This means that it must come from an animal which chews the cud and has a cloven hoof, or from domesticated poultry which has been slaughtered and handled according to ritual. Meat of the pig, rabbit and birds of prey is forbidden, as are products containing their fats, milk or eggs. Fish needs to have both fins and scales to be kosher.

⌘ Milk and meat are not eaten at the same meal. (If meat is eaten first, then the person should wait for three hours before drinking milk or eating other dairy products. If milk or dairy products are eaten first, then the person need only wait for half an hour.)

The Sabbath

⌘ The Sabbath may be strictly observed. Adherents may not undertake any creative work. This may include; travelling by vehicle, using the telephone or money and switching electrical appliances on and off.

⌘ This has obvious implications for nursing care when planning discharges and for the use of the nurse call system.

Dying

⌘ Jewish law forbids the hastening of death.

⌘ The dying Jew may wish to hear or recite the *Shema* (declaration of belief in God). Some may wish to make confession.

⌘ A dying Jew should not be moved or left alone.

⌘ Jews believe in life after death. An Orthodox Jew believes in physical resurrection and will not agree to organ donation or donation for research. Liberal and Reform Jews believe that the soul survives independently and may agree to donation.

Post-mortems

⌘ Post-mortems are not permitted in Jewish law, except where civil law demands it.

Procedure to be followed in the event of the death of a Jewish patient

⌘ Traditionally the body should remain untouched for ten minutes.

⌘ Remove all tubes from the body (unless referral to coroner/post-mortem).

⌘ The patient's eyes should be closed by a child of the deceased if possible.

⌘ The body should be handled as little as possible by staff.

⌘ If necessary, the arms and hands may be laid straight by sides.

⌘ Clothing present on the body should remain and the deceased should be covered with a clean white sheet.

⌘ In the first instance, contact the Jewish chaplain. The Jewish chaplain cannot be contacted after sunset on Fridays until after dark on Saturdays and on certain religious festivals. In this event the hospital chaplain on call may be contacted.

⌘ Wherever possible the deceased should remain in the bed until the Sabbath or Festival has terminated. If this is not possible the deceased may be moved to the hospital mortuary, although staff should be instructed that the body should be handled and moved as little as possible.

⌘ Washing is to be carried out by the Jewish Burial Society under the direction of the Jewish chaplain.

Sikhism

Sikhism was founded in India by Guru Nanak. It is younger than Hinduism and is based on the teachings of Ten Gurus.

Sikhism is based on one God, with great importance given to worship of, and to a personal relationship with, God. Its faith is a combination of elements of both Hindu and Muslim beliefs but tends to be more flexible.

The followers of Sikhism, Sikhs, believe in reincarnation but reject the notion of caste on the grounds that all people are equal. Many worship in a Gurdwara – a Sikh Temple (place of Guru).

The Holy Book is the Guru Granth Sahab, a collection of the writings of the Ten Gurus.

The five signs significant to Sikhism (five Ks)

Kara: a metal bangle which is usually not removed, worn by men and women (sign of eternity).

Kesh and keski: uncut hair and turban.

Kangha: the comb (sign of cleanliness). Used to secure long hair under a turban.

Kirpan: a small symbolic dagger (sign of strength).

Kaccha: a sacred undergarment or pair of shorts (sign of action and goodness).

Taking 'Amrit' is special devotion in Sikhism. Sikhs who undertake this are known as 'Amrit Dari'.

They promise to wear the five signs of Sikhism, carry on special prayers, not eat meat, and attend the Gurdwara every day.

Main points affecting nursing care

Birth

⌘ Similar to Hindu.

Abortion/family planning

⌘ Often same problems about contraception and abortion apply as to Hindus.

Transfusions

⌘ Generally accepted.

Diet

⌘ Beef forbidden. May be vegetarian.

P.

⌘ :stly and will be unwilling to expose
. chaperone should always be provided.
be inappropriate.

⌘ :. :p their hair covered at all times.

Pro   ***the event of the death of a Sikh***
patie

⌘ For   ; should not be removed in life or death
  unle: iry: they should be left intact and hair
  shoul   air and beard must not be trimmed. Eyes
  shou.d   ported and limbs straightened. The face
  shou.d :   .ightened to give an expression of peace.
  Cover \   vith no religious emblems.

⌘ There are   hism. Words from the Guru Grant Sahib
  may be re.   ly, or temple (*Gurdwara*) reader. Any
  practising Si.   ifort. No last rites although the dying
person should be encouraged to utter 'Waheguru, Waheguru'
(Wonderful Lord, Wonderful Lord).

⌘ Traditionally, the family will want to wash and lay out the body
for themselves – they should be offered the opportunity to do this
at ward level if they would like to.

⌘ There are no religious objections to other people touching the body.

Other religious faiths and beliefs

Christian Science

The Church aims to 'reinstate primitive Christianity and its lost
element of healing'. The Church is primarily concerned with spiritual
regeneration and redemption from sin. There is a strong belief in the
power of prayer for healing sickness and disease. Some Christian
Scientists may defer to family pressure to undergo conventional
medical treatment but most will seek care in a Christian Science
nursing home if possible. However, following accidents or because
of legal/family pressure, they may be in hospital. During pregnancy,
childbirth and for their children, when the law insists, they will
accept conventional medicine.

Main points affecting nursing care

Prayer

⌘ Prayer is silent and although privacy would be appreciated, it is not vital. Access to the Bible and the textbook *Science and Health with Key to the Scripture* and other Christian Science literature is important.

Diet

⌘ Alcohol and tobacco are forbidden.

Post-mortems

⌘ These are not approved of, nor is donation of the body for research purposes.

Blood transfusion/organ donation

⌘ A Christian Scientist will not normally accept or donate blood or organs.

⌘ No special requirements after death.

⌘ It is preferred that the body of a female is handled by female staff.

The Church of Jesus Christ of Latter-day Saints (the Mormon church)

The Book of Mormon (revelations of many prophets) is central to the belief and is as important as the Old and New Testaments. The Mormon Church believes that the Holy Trinity (Father, Son and Holy Ghost) are three separate members of the Godhead.

Mormons believe in a spirit life prior to birth, and that the spirit returns to a spiritual place following death. At some point in the future the body and spirit will be reunited.

Those Mormons who are considered worthy may undergo a special ceremony of 'endowment' at the temple. Death is considered a temporary sadness as the family will be reunited at the resurrection.

Main points affecting nursing care

Diet

⌘ Mormons are not usually vegetarians, but eat meat sparingly and avoid blood products such as black pudding.

⌘ Alcohol, tobacco, tea and coffee are forbidden. Acceptable alternatives are milk, water or fruit juice.

Hygiene/privacy

⌘ A sacred undergarment will be worn by those who have undergone endowment. This is removable for hygiene purposes, and for washing, but is a very private item and should be worn at all times, even after death. If the garment must be removed it should be treated with great respect and not left open to public view.

Dying

⌘ Members of the Melchizedek priesthood may be called to give 'blessing', but there are no other rituals to be observed.

⌘ No special requirements after death except that the sacred undergarment, if worn, must be replaced after the last office is complete.

Humanism

In 1963 the British Humanist Association was formed. They do not accept God, but have an outlook of goodwill, and respect for everyone regardless of colour, creed and class. Humanists may have distinct needs based on the philosophy of humanism. These may feature as follows:

Meaning and purpose

Humanists try to find meaning and purpose in life. They may rely on scientific testing, reasoning and discussion to arrive at facts.

Belief in the overall quality of life

Humanists believe that it is the overall quality of life that is important. They give consideration to the point that all people have natural potential for understanding, caring and co-operation, and an awareness of the consequences of their actions. These, they believe, motivate us to form relationships and govern behaviour towards others. Humanists believe that we should use these qualities to make life better for all of us.

Humanists tend to follow the 'golden rule':

Treat other people as you would like them to treat you.

Incidentally, this is shared by all of the world's main religious faiths. The two fundamental moral principles of Humanists are:

❖ Happiness.

❖ Tolerance.

Reasoning and rights

Humanists share a common ground on moral problems, but give consideration to all possible consequences when discussing policies for action. The humanists hold beliefs in birth control and abortion, equal rights for everyone, voluntary euthanasia and freedom of speech which are all dealt in this way.

Many people find humanism as an alternative to a 'theistic' or God-centred-religion. In this respect, humanists play a part in multi-faith groups such as the Religious Education Council, to represent the views of non-theistic people.

Main points affecting nursing care

Food

⌘ Many are vegetarians, but not all.

Blood transfusion and organ transplant

⌘ There are usually no objections to these, but it remains a subject to be dealt with sensitively.

Death and dying

⌘ There are no particular rites for a dying patient. Privacy and dignity, as with all patients, is required.

⌘ Routine last offices are appropriate, and both cremation and burial are acceptable.

Jehovah's Witnesses

Jehovah's Witnesses are an international body of Christians. The modern movement was begun by Charles Russell in the USA in the 1870s. There are now more than five million Jehovah's Witnesses world-wide with over 120,000 in the UK.

Beliefs

Jehovah's Witnesses believe that the Bible is the word of God and accept everything written in it as true. They believe that the word 'God' is merely a title and that, in the Bible, God reveals his own personal name, Jehovah. Jesus Christ is seen as Jehovah's son. Witnesses do not view themselves as preaching from their own understanding, but as pointing out what the Bible says and honouring Jehovah by letting him speak. They believe that planet earth was created to be mankind's home for ever and that all people, the living and resurrected dead who accept Jesus, will live here in Paradise after Judgement Day. However, they also believe that there is a Heaven and that 144,000 chosen people will go there to be with its King, Jesus, in his Heavenly Kingdom where their role will be to govern and to administer the affairs of those living on earth.

Baptism

Witnesses do not baptise their babies or young children. When a teenager is thought to be old enough to understand what baptism means or when a newly converted person reaches a similar understanding, they are baptised by total immersion in water. This is viewed as a public statement that their lives are now dedicated to God and marks their ordination as ministers.

Holidays and celebrations

Children of Jehovah's Witnesses do not participate in religious holiday observances or festivals such as Christmas, Easter and Halloween. They do not celebrate birthdays, New Year's Day, Valentine's Day, May Day or Mother's Day. The giving and receiving of presents takes place at any time of the year. Most Jehovah's Witness parents are very conscious of the possible accusation of depriving their children and provide plenty of compensatory recreation and pleasure activities on other non-festival occasions.

Death and bereavement

Witnesses believe the whole person is a soul. They believe, therefore, that when a person dies, the soul dies and that death is a state of unconsciousness from which believers will be awakened by resurrection when Jesus comes again. There are no special rituals for the sick or dying. Funerals are conducted by an appointed minister of Jehovah's Witnesses.

Unless there is compelling reason, such as when a post-mortem is required by a governmental agency, Jehovah's Witnesses generally prefer that the body of a beloved relative not be subjected to post-mortem dissection. The appropriate close relative(s) can decide if a limited post-mortem is advisable to determine cause of death.

Main points affecting nursing care

Blood, blood products and blood transfusions

⌘ Jehovah's Witnesses refusal of blood is well known and well documented. They believe that taking blood into the body is forbidden by Biblical passages such as Genesis 9:3,4; Leviticus 17:13,14; and Acts 15:19–21, which equate blood with life or 'soul'. They believe such texts establish the sacredness of blood and rule out its use in transfusions of whole blood, packed red blood cells, platelets, white blood cells and plasma. Some Witnesses will accept the use of minor blood fractions such as albumin, clotting factors and immunoglobulins (see 'Immunisation and vaccination', below). Most Witnesses are knowledgeable about the hazards of blood therapies. Recombinant forms of blood fractions, when available, are likely to be viewed as preferable.

⌘ Jehovah's Witnesses carry on their person an advanced medical directive/release that directs no blood transfusions be given under any circumstances, while releasing medical practitioners from responsibility for any damages that might arise because of their refusal of blood. Appropriate consent/release forms stating matters similarly and dealing more specifically with the hospital care needed can be signed on admission.

Autotransfusion, pre-deposited blood and autologous techniques

⌘ Jehovah's Witnesses believe that blood removed from the body should be disposed of so they do not accept surgical techniques involving storage of blood by pre-deposit. However, many witnesses will permit the use of haemodialysis, heart/lung and perioperative blood salvage systems (non-blood primed), where the extra-corporeal circulation is uninterrupted and a closed circuit with the patient's own circulatory system is maintained.

Immunisation and vaccination

⌘ Inoculation by vaccine (toxoid) usually should cause no problem. All the Jehovah's Witness patient will need is reassurance that the injection is not prepared from blood.

⌘ The use of albumin in the preparation of some inoculations, such as measles, mumps, and rubella (MMR), might trouble the conscience of some and lead to refusal. Similar difficulties may arise when a vaccination is proposed using serum (antitoxin), where the preparation has been made from immunoglobulin. Because blood fractions are involved, some Jehovah's Witnesses will not accept these injections for themselves or their children. Others will view the matter differently, perceiving the blood fraction involved as being so small and so unlike actual blood as not to trouble their conscience at all. The latter will accept the injection. If recombinant forms are available no problem will arise.

Organ donation and transplantation

⌘ Because the Bible places no specific ban on the taking in of tissue or bone from another human, Witnesses regard the acceptance of an organ transplant as a personal, medical decision. The same is true of an organ donation.

Prolongation of life and the right to die

⌘ Jehovah's Witnesses refusal of blood is not connected to a belief in 'the right to die'. They hold life as sacred and believe that reasonable and humane effort should be made to sustain and prolong life. However, their reading of the scriptures leads them to believe that no extraordinary, complicated, distressing and costly measures have to be taken to sustain a person, if in the general consensus of the attending medical practitioners, it would merely prolong the dying process and/or leave the patient with no quality of life. Advance directives by the patient defining what is or is not wanted should be respected.

⌘ When the doctor believes that a blood transfusion is essential, the hospital liaison committee should be consulted. The hospital liaison committee (HLC) is a group of trained professionals with up-to-date information on non-blood medical management techniques being practised in hospital facilities around the world. By consulting the HLC an acceptable therapy can often be found that respects the adult patient's legal rights.

Treatment of children

In the event of medical staff wishing to continue with a blood transfusion for a minor child, the following should be considered:

⌘ Jehovah's Witnesses are not opposed to medical treatment, only blood transfusion.

⌘ Has the hospital liaison committee been contacted for assistance?

⌘ Does a true emergency exist?

⌘ Have the parents been given the opportunity to express their views?

⌘ Has treatment with alternative non-blood management been fully explored?

⌘ Have the hazards of using blood been fully considered?

⌘ Has an attempt been made to reach an understanding with the parents about the circumstances in which it is proposed to transfuse the child?

If it is necessary to seek legal sanction for the proposed action, a specific issue order should be applied for and the medical social worker contacted. Efforts should be made to limit any order to the specific medical condition requiring treatment with the parents being kept informed at each stage of the application. If parents have refused consent and the decision is taken to continue, the nurse **should not** administer the blood to the child but expect that the doctor will do so. A doctor's freedom to act on his own judgement alone in defiance of parental views is strictly limited to emergency treatment.

⌘ The nurse caring for the child must ensure that all activity is accurately documented in the care plan.

Hospital liaison committee

Jehovah's Witnesses and the medical profession co-operate

Jehovah's Witnesses are not against medical treatment. They do, however, take a firm, non-negotiable stand against the use of blood, based on their understanding of scriptural law. In recent years this scriptural stand has been steadily vindicated by a flood of new scientific findings on both the dangers of homologous transfusions and the efficacy of alternatives to transfusion.

To bring this information to the attention of the medical community a world-wide network of hospital liaison committees (HLCs) has been set up, based on major cities with large medical institutions. In Britain, there are 36 committees with an average of five ministers on each. Their work has a number of aspects.

⌘ Each HLC member has been trained to help Jehovah's Witnesses when they meet problems involving blood.

⌘ Visits are made to medical facilities to meet administrators, doctors and nursing staff to encourage the continuation and expansion of the treatment of Jehovah's Witnesses without using blood.

⌘ Articles from a wide range of prestigious international medical journals are made available to doctors and surgeons to acquaint them with what can be done without resorting to blood transfusions.

⌘ In cases where there is some special need, appropriate articles are faxed directly to the medical facility to help physicians treat Jehovah's Witnesses without using blood.

⌘ The committee can arrange for consultation with other co-operative doctors to develop strategies for bloodless treatment or surgery.

⌘ Local HLCs are part of a world-wide network of 1,000 committees covering 230 countries, with over 5,000 doctors world-wide available for consultation/transfer. On-line medical researchers with access to 4,000 journals operate the medical article distribution service.

⌘ HLC services are available on 24-hour call.

In all these activities, the aims are to work co-operatively with the medical profession and to avoid confrontation, personal trauma for the patient and clinical/nursing staff, and unwanted publicity. Each HLC has a patient visitation group. This is a group of ministers appointed to visit and care for the spiritual needs of hospitalised Jehovah's Witnesses. Each minister is assigned to a local hospital and is known and recognised by that hospital's administration.

Paganism

Paganism is probably among the oldest surviving religions, and was in existence long before other current major world religions. It has no equivalent to the Bible or Holy Book as all of its writings were destroyed, therefore their traditions have been passed on verbally. There are many variations within Paganism as within other religions. There are, however, common fundamentals.

The feminine principle

This is the Goddess who is the main focus of worship. She can also be known by other names, and can be seen as maiden, mother and crone – youth, maturity and death. The masculine principle or a God is also acknowledged.

The belief in freedom but with responsibility

It is believed that everything a person does will return but be greater and more concentrated. Many lead 'alternative lifestyles' to emphasise their relationship with nature.

A belief in destiny

While not removing responsibility, this acknowledges that there are some things outside of their control.

A form of reincarnation

It is believed that the equivalent of a soul, is released back to the Earth following decay. It is seen as the recycling of energy.

A close relationship

All things are treated with respect, as it is believed with nature that all things have a spirit, including rocks, plants etc.

Pagans may be reluctant to disclose their beliefs, in view of publicity about ritual child abuse. However, this publicity is not based on fact and leads to a lot of misconceptions.

Main points affecting nursing care

Food

⌘ Many Pagans are vegetarians, but not all. Some may eat pork at Christmas.

Blood transfusion/organ donation

⌘ There are no religious objections to these and it is an individual's decision.

Death and dying

⌘ It is important for Pagans to have information that will enable them to prepare for death. Unless asked for, a visit by the Hospital chaplain would not be appropriate; they have their own spiritual advisers. Unless otherwise requested, last offices can be carried out as usual.

⌘ Both burial and cremation are acceptable, but the funeral will be conducted by the person's own spiritual adviser or by other Pagans.

Rastafarianism

Rastafarianism, a recent religion, was founded in the 1930s and is strongest in Jamaica but has spread to other African-Caribbean communities, particularly in the USA and Europe. When Ras (Prince) Tafari was enthroned in Ethiopia in the 1930s as Emperor Haile Selassie, he was hailed as the black messiah who was predicted earlier to arrive in Africa.

Rastafarians accept some of the teachings of the Bible as it is the tradition of Ethiopia, believing that God took human form, as Christ first, then as Ras Tafari. Rastafarians draw similarities with

Israelites in that they liken the fate of all black people in the West to that of Israelites enslaved in Egypt and Babylon, and believe that they will not be free unless they return to Africa. This is interpreted by many Rastafarians as a spiritual state of mind.

Main points affecting nursing care

⌘ Both men and women are easily identifiable by their 'dreadlocks' which are a symbol of faith (but not all dreadlocks wearers are Rastafarians). Orthodox Rastafarians will not permit their hair to be cut, and may wish to keep their hair covered.

⌘ Rastafarian women dress modestly and there is a taboo on the wearing of second-hand clothes so the orthodox Rastafarian may prefer to wear a disposable theatre gown. It is believed to be very important to visit the sick and this often occurs in groups.

Diet

⌘ All forms of pig meat are forbidden, as are foods cooked in pig fat. Many Rastafarians are vegetarian. Some fish are thought to be unwholesome (such as herring and sardine). Fresh organic food is usually preferred to canned.

Marijuana (Ganja) is seen as the holy herb:

And the earth brought forth grass and herbs yielding seed after his kind, and God saw that it was good.

Genesis 1:2

Better is a dinner of herb where love is, than a stalled ox and hatred therewith.

Proverbs 15:17

He caused the grass to grow for the cattle, and the herb for the service of man.

Psalm 104:14

However, not every Rastafarian smokes.

Dying patient

⌘ Ratafarianism is a personal religion. Believers have a deep love of God and believe he is present wherever people are.

⌘ There are no church buildings, set services or official clergy. All members of the faith share in its religious aspects and they may wish to pray with a dying patient. Families may also require the presence of a religious leader. They believe in resurrection of the soul but not the flesh. Routine last offices are appropriate.

Post-mortems

⌘ Many Rastafarians would dislike the idea of post-mortem or donation of the body for research. You will need to ask.

⌘ Burial is preferred and in some cases the body may be flown back to the country of origin.

Blood transfusion/organ donation

⌘ Fear of contamination may prevent the acceptance of blood transfusion. However, donation to, and reception from, a family member may be acceptable.

⌘ Fear of contamination and a belief that organ donation constitutes interference with God's plan may prevent this.

Other considerations

⌘ Some Rastafarians may not be willing to receive treatments of Western medicine, and prefer herbalism, homeopathy and other alternative treatments instead. Again, check with the patient and family first.

Seventh Day Adventists (SDA)

Followers of this religion observe Saturday as the Sabbath (the Seventh Day). The Bible is accepted as infallible, and they live a life of strict temperance.

The Sabbath lasts from sunset on Friday until sunset on Saturday. It is a day for communion with God, and is kept for rest and worship.

Principles of the faith

God is seen as the Creator, Jesus Christ as the Saviour and the Holy Spirit as the Comforter. Other principles include:

❖ Salvation by grace through faith.

❖ The imminent return of the Lord.

❖ The Ten Commandments and the example of Jesus as the standards of conduct.

❖ The gifts of the Holy Spirit to the church.

❖ Healthful living, remembering that our bodies are temples of the Holy Ghost.

❖ The mortality of man and resurrection of the saved to eternal life at Christ's return.

❖ Observing the Ordinance of Humility and the Lord's Supper.

❖ Baptism by immersion.

❖ The return of one-tenth of income to the Lord.

❖ The support of the Gospel by willing missionary service and gifts as the Lord prospers them.

❖ Avoiding worldliness in our deportment, recreation, and attire.

❖ Loyalty to the church and its organisation, refraining from any word or deed that might tarnish its fair name.

Main points affecting nursing care

Prayer needs

⌘ There is no set time for praying and there are no rituals attached to prayer time. All that is required is a calm, peaceful environment and the privacy of screens (if in an open plan ward) or preferably a side ward.

⌘ Adventists usually like a short period, at the beginning and end of the day, when they can spend time reflecting and communicating or talking to their Lord. As part of this quiet meditation a passage of scripture from the Bible is read or some other devotional text, prior to quietly and reverently praying.

⌘ Adventist patients will pray by themselves, but if visited by a fellow Adventist he/she rarely leaves without saying a comforting prayer of encouragement for the patient.

Privacy/hygiene needs

⌘ Again there are no rituals associated with privacy and hygiene needs. Simply observe the usual social conventions afforded to adults: respect the dignity of the individual and ensure that vulnerable, frail individuals are protected from unnecessary exposure when daily ablutions or bathing is carried out.

Diet

⌘ Adventists are very health conscious in their eating habits, and so do not eat 'unclean meat', such as pork or pork products (eg. ham, bacon, sausages, pork pies, pâté or lard). Shellfish such as crab, lobster, clams and prawns are also forbidden foods. Stimulants are avoided including tea, coffee and alcohol.

⌘ Some Adventists are vegetarians, and their diet is based around nuts and pulses for the second class proteins, plenty of fruit and vegetables, fruit juices, milk/soya milk, herbal or fruit tea, barley cup or decaffeinated coffee.

Care required by the terminally ill or dying Adventist

⌘ A calm and peaceful environment is essential to enable quiet contemplation. A bright and cheerful side room, filled with flowers (God's simple and beautiful creation) will help to 'lift the spirits'. A side room will permit not only privacy and rest, but also the opportunity for the dying person's family and minister/pastor to have unrestricted access and quality time with the dying loved one and friend.

⌘ Some Adventist relatives may volunteer or wish to carry out loving personal acts such as bed bathing or freshening up, combing the hair, shaving facial hair or feeding/giving fluids to the patient. Such acts are intended to make the dying person feel cherished, comfortable and cared for, as well as giving relatives and friends something practical to do. When death is imminent, close relatives, supported by the minister, will often stay with the dying person. They may sing the favourite songs of the dying person or read their favourite Psalms or other Biblical text. The minister will lead the prayers that are intended to comfort and relieve the dying person as their life forces ebb away.

Fellowship

⌘ When a fellow Adventist is ill and admitted to hospital, often church 'brothers' and 'sisters' are keen to visit. This sometimes leads to misunderstandings with the nursing staff, if large numbers of church members descend on the ward at visiting times or keep phoning the ward staff for frequent bulletins. A little tactful diplomacy will help. If the nurse-in-charge negotiates with either the patient's minister or next-of-kin to communicate with them only and then they, in turn, can pass on appropriate amounts of information to the church members at the weekly meetings. For prolonged periods of hospitalisation, the ward staff will have to be flexible and use their discretion when dealing with large numbers of visitors for one patient. (As the visitors are keen to show their concern and pay their respects.) The nursing staff perhaps should inform the visitors that a limited number of visitors should be at the patient's bedside at any one time.

Summary

This chapter gives the opportunity to gain some insights into some of the religions encountered in practice. Also, specific religious and spiritual needs of patients of various faiths are outlined. The information gained from the previous chapter and this section should be sufficient for formulation of care plans related to spiritual care. However, certain skills are necessary for the provision of spiritual care as part of an holistic approach to nursing patients. These skills are identified and developed in the next chapter.

References

Murray RB, Zentner JB (1989) *Nursing Concepts for Health Promotion.* Prentice Hall, London

McAvoy BR, Donaldson LJ (eds) (1990) *Health Care For Asians.* Oxford Medical Publications, Oxford

Narayanasamy A, Andrews A (2000) Cultural impact of Islam on the future directions of nurse education. *Nurse Educ Today* **26**: 57–64

Narayanasamy A, Daly P (1998) *Spiritual, Religious and Cultural Care: A resource package.* Queens Medical Centre, University of Nottingham

Annotated bibliography

Readers wishing further insights into major religions and religious needs may find the following useful:

Carson, VB (1989) *Spiritual Dimensions of Nursing Practice*. WB Sanders, London

Chapter four provides insights into Western spirituality and health care. Readers looking for perpectives on Eastern spirituality may find chapter five useful. A balanced discussion is provided on issues related to religious beliefs, legal issues and health care in chapter six

Murray RB, Zenner RB (1989) *Nursing Concepts for Health Promotion*. Prentice Hall, London

Chapter nine is particularly relevant and provides insights into Hinduism, Buddhism and Shintoism, Confusianism and Taoism, Islam, Judaism, Christianity, Protestantism and other groups of interest.

McGilloway O, Myco F (1985) *Nursing and Spiritual Care*. Harper and Row, London

Chapter one focuses on religions, magic and medicine as well as spiritual needs from an historical overview. Chapter two introduces the reader to religious beliefs, practices and philosophies. Chapter three is particularly useful for insights into the philosophies of non-believers in the health care situation. Chapter six looks at the Christian patient and the role of the chaplain. Chapter seven provides the Jewish perspective, chapter eight the Hindu perspective and the Muslim perspective is included in chapter nine.

Pearson J, Roberts, RH, Samuel G (1999) *Nature Religion Today: Paganism in the Modern World*. Edinburgh University Press, Edinburgh

An authorative book on Paganism. It portrays Paganism as growing at an unprecendented rate while traditional religions are on the decline. It gives accounts of its believers, environment activism, feminism, spoils of capitalism and innovative forms of spirituality, such as dedication to the Goddess.

Shelly JA, Fish S (1988) *Spiritual Care: The Nurses Role*. Inter Varsity Press, Illinois

This book is committed to spirituality from a Christian perspective and provides a comprehensive insight into spiritual care.

The following books also provide detailed coverage of the various cultural and religious groups in the UK. Although they all comprise similar information related to the above they take a different approach.

Henley A, Schott J (1999) *Culture, Religion and Patient Care in a Multi-Ethnic Society*. Age Concern, London

Karmi G (1996) *The Ethnic Health Handbook: A factfile for health care professionals*. Blackwell Science, Oxford

Sheikh A, Gatrad A (eds) (2000) *Caring for Muslim Patients*. Radcliffe Medical Press, Oxford

5

Skills development for spiritual care

Although a sufficient knowledge about spiritual needs is necessary, skills of self-awareness, communication skills such as listening, trust building and giving hope, and client education need to be developed to equip the nurse to assist in meeting a client's spiritual needs.

Self-awareness

Before we instigate effective spiritual care, we must know and understand our level of spiritual awareness. An examination of our personal beliefs and values is a necessary part of spiritual care (Narayanasamy, 1998). The nurse who has a positive attitude to spiritual health is likely to be sensitive to any problem a client has concerning spirituality. A continuous examination of our own personal spiritual beliefs, enables each nurse to appreciate that everybody does not share the same outlook. An awareness of our own prejudices and bias would ensure that we do not impose our own values and beliefs on others, especially spiritual doctrines. Self-awareness enables us to adopt a non-judgemental approach and avoid taking any steps that could lead to accusations of proselytising. It is likely that a person who has developed self-awareness will show more tolerance, acceptance and respect for another person's spirituality.

Self-awareness is a skill that has to be acquired and continuously developed. It is an acknowledgement of our own feelings and behaviours, and ability to accept and understand these in ourselves. It can be elaborated as an acknowledgement of our:

* values, attitudes, prejudices, beliefs, assumptions, and feelings
* personal motives and needs and the extent to which these are being met
* degree of attention to others
* genuineness and investment of self, and how the above might have an effect on others
* the intentional and unconscious use of self.

It is widely acknowledged that a training in self-awareness is a fundamental process before we understand others. According to Burnard (1990), to become aware of, and to have deeper understanding of ourselves is to have a sharper and clearer picture of what is happening to others. Limited awareness of ourselves may mean remaining blind to others. The first step to being self-aware is to examine ourselves.

We can develop self-awareness by various means. However, the methods used for increasing our awareness must contain the facets of an inner search and observations of others.

One simple method of enhancing self-awareness is the process of noticing what we are doing, the process of self-monitoring; this involves staying conscious of what you are doing and what is happening to you. To put it another way, 'stay awake' and develop the skill of keeping your attention focused on your actions, both verbal and non-verbal.

Assessment of our present understanding of knowledge, skills and the learning of new materials, skills and techniques will be heavily influenced by our degree of self-awareness. We are likely to lose control of our self-development if we remain blind to the need to increase our self-awareness. Without self-awareness we cannot:

- be in control of our own development
- identify key performance areas
- analyse our own performance, or identify concrete objectives
- make action plans to help our own development
- monitor our own progress.

An increase in our self-awareness is not only the beginning of wisdom but also the growth of our personal and professional effectiveness.

We can foster an attitude to increase our self-awareness by evaluating ourselves by asking questions such as:

❖ How much time do I invest in reflecting about myself?

❖ How reassured am I that I have a reasonable understanding of myself?

❖ How do I see myself, and how do I feel about myself?

❖ What are my significant strengths and weaknesses?

❖ Do I really face up to the truth about myself, or do I try to evade the truth about me from myself?

Other methods of developing self-awareness are through introspection, through experience and through feedback.

Introspection

Meditation and yoga can be a useful way of developing self-awareness using the introspection method. Simple breathing and meditation techniques are sufficient for this purpose. Meditation and yoga serve another useful purpose in that these techniques can be useful methods of dealing with job-related stress. Becoming aware of, and consciously noting experiences are other means of introspection. To complement these processes the following are useful: identifying past and present prejudices; identifying past and present approaches to personal problem-solving.

Experience

Self-awareness is also developed through experience. The experiential method is a useful method of learning through experience. Participation in experiential exercises brings the desirable increase in self-awareness.

Self-awareness through feedback

Self-awareness cannot be developed by adhering solely to the introspection and experiential methods alone. Introspection and experiential exercises will give us some understanding of ourselves, but complete self-awareness requires knowledge about behaviour too; for this we require the help of others: it takes two to know one fully.

I am aware of my inner feelings (inner processes) but sometimes I cannot see my behaviour. Another person can see my behaviour, but is not aware of my inner feelings and experience. I can see the other person's behaviour, but not his inner experience.

For complete self-awareness, then, we need to strengthen the knowledge gained by introspecting with knowledge obtained by feedback from others about our behaviour.

Self-disclosure is a fundamental part of self-awareness and it has three characteristics:

* being subjectively true

* making personal statements about yourself
* intentionally revealing yourself to another person.

Self-disclosure involves the process of revealing information about yourself: your ideas, values, and feelings that are similar to the ones experienced by those you are is trying to help.

There is significant clinical evidence to suggest that a nurse's self-disclosure increases the likelihood of the client's self-disclosure (Stuart and Sundeen, 1983). Self-disclosure results in a successful therapeutic outcome. However, our self-disclosure must be handled judiciously, and this is determined by the quality, quantity, and appropriateness of what we reveal. We must handle our disclosure sensitively so that clients feel comfortable enough to tell us something about themselves. If nurses reveal very little about themselves, this may reduce the client's willingness to talk about themselves, and conversely, too many disclosures may decrease the time available for the client to talk or even alienate him/her.

Communication skills

Good communication skills are a 'must' for spiritual care. The most essential communication skill in spiritual care is active listening without being judgemental. The points about self-awareness mentioned earlier are necessary for developing non-judgemental attitudes.

Non-judgemental means unconditional acceptance of others. To have faith, trust and respect for another person despite his behaviour is often a difficult quality to achieve, but with increasing self-awareness this can be developed. A non-judgemental approach is acceptance of an individual without any kind of judgement, without criticism, and without reservation. This not only requires complete acceptance of a person, but respect for him/her without necessarily knowing what the previous behaviour has been, or who he/she is.

As pointed out earlier when providing spiritual care, we must reserve or detach ourselves from our own personal values, ideals or beliefs. Clients should feel that we are genuinely interested, that we want to know them and how they think and feel, and that we do not judge them. Such a relationship, which encourages clients to believe that someone else is interested in and cares for them and that they are valued as unique individuals, means that they are far more likely to have a positive image of themselves.

Genuineness is a quality based on the person's ability to be him/herself. It means being honest and open about expressing feelings and not just persons who act the role of nurses. Again, self-awareness is a means by which this quality can be developed. It demands honesty and courage to be allowed to be seen as a real person.

Active listening is important because its purpose is to enable the client to be at ease and to make use of the listening process in such a way that the listener can help the client deal with spiritual needs and experience further spiritual growth. The active listener acts as a talking mirror, encouraging and reflecting back to the client what the listener hears, sees, or senses.

The rudiments of being a good listener are:

❖ The nurse needs to create the right kind of climate in which the person requiring spiritual care feels accepted and confident enough to be able to talk about his spiritual thoughts and feelings.

❖ The client needs to feel that the nurse is listening to what he is saying and what he is feeling and not only listening, but accepting and understanding him. All this ties up with responding to people in ways which are helpful.

❖ Good listening is really paying close attention to what someone is saying and this is essential, but it is not easy. We need to suspend our thoughts and give the other person our complete attention.

❖ We can demonstrate understanding by reflecting the client's thoughts back, showing that we are listening hard, that we are making a real effort to understand what the client is thinking and feeling.

❖ Make the client feel that it is all right to go on talking, that their feelings are being accepted. State that you are genuinely interested in what the client is saying, and respond warmly.

Trust building

Trust is necessary because confidence in the nurse-client relationship is vital in spiritual care and, indeed, to the well-being of the client. Trust between nurse and client develops over time as the client tests the environment, risks self-disclosure, and observes the nurse's adherence to commitment. The following approach enhances initial trust:

- listening attentively to the client's feeling
- responding to the client's feelings
- demonstrating consistency, especially keeping appointments and promises
- viewing the situation from the client's perspective.

An increasing level of self-awareness of personal feelings, along the lines suggested earlier, on the part of the nurse also enhances trust. It enables the client to disclose uncomfortable, even forbidden, feelings in safety. The nurse must continue to build on the trust already gained by being reliable. Reliability is one other factor that strengthens and sustains a trusting relationship. Reliability is measured in terms of the nurse's commitment to the spiritual needs of the client and this means promises and adherence to nursing care plans must be carried out promptly and followed through.

Giving hope

Hope is something that we cannot easily give to another, but every effort can be made to support and encourage the hoping abilities of a client. Nurses are often in ideal positions to foster or hinder hope. A caring relationship can be offered that permits, rather than stifles, the efforts of the client to develop hope. The nurse can support the person who is testing his own beliefs or struggling with questions of fear and faith. Further encouragement can be given to the clients to talk about their fears. Helping clients to relive their memory is another way of facilitating hoping. Memories of events when life's needs were met, when despair was overcome and when failure was defeated, can all be used to encourage a client to take a fresh view and face the future with confidence as part of spiritual recovery.

Herth (1990) identifies hope-fostering strategies which could be used as part of spiritual care. She defines hope-fostering strategies as, 'those sources that function to instil, support or restore hope by facilitating the hoping process in some way' (p. 1253). The following can be utilised as hope fostering strategies.

Interpersonal connectedness

A meaningful and shared relationship with close ones and others (including nurses) is said to be a feature of interpersonal connectedness. For example, an harmonious and supportive relationship within the family offers the client hope and strength, fundamental parts of a person's spirituality. The willingness of a nurse to share in a client's hopes is a feature of this strategy.

Light-heartedness

The features of this are feelings of delight, joy or playfulness that are communicated verbally or non-verbally. The nurse can foster light-heartedness among clients. The spirit of light-heartedness can provide a communication link between persons and a way of coping with deterioration in body function and confused emotions; it can provide a sense of release from the present moment.

Personal attributes

The nurse can enable clients to maximise their determination, courage and serenity. A search for a sense of inner peace, harmony and calm is one way of enabling the client to achieve serenity.

Attainable aims

A characteristic of such aims is the direction of efforts towards some purpose. The presence of aims often fosters hope. The nurse who helps clients to search for meaning and purpose in life would actually foster hope. A sense of meaning and purpose in life also gives hope. Helping a client to redefine his aims and channelling his thoughts on to other events or significant others are useful strategies of hope-fostering.

Spiritual base

The presence of active spiritual beliefs (in God or a 'higher being') and spiritual practices is a source of hope. These can enable clients to participate in specific practices. These may include: praying; enlisting the prayers of others; listening to spiritual music and spiritual programmes on the radio or television, in religious activities; maintaining specific religious customs; and visiting members and leaders of their spiritual community.

Uplifting memories

Recalling uplifting memories/times is another hope-fostering strategy. The nurse can help clients to share happy stories from the past and to reminisce through old picture albums. Reliving positive activities from the past, such as an enjoyable holiday, significant events (birth of child, receipt of medal) and 'sunset over mountains', can serve to renew the hoping process. It is most likely that memories of past events can serve to enrich the present moment.

Affirmation of worth

Having our own individuality accepted, honoured and acknowledged can foster hope. Nurses, family and friends can be party to a client's feeling of self-worth as a dignified human being. This can be uplifting and act as a source of hope.

Client education

The client needs to grow spiritually to achieve a full status of health. Good health orientation includes body, mind, spirit and the additional consideration of cultural background. This can be achieved when a nurse creates a relationship in which nurse-client education takes place. The client needs to be educated to develop the hoping strategy. Trusting is another skill that can be learned and the nurse can provide opportunities for the client to develop this aspect of the relationship.

The client needs a learning opportunity to gain insights into his own spiritual awareness. He needs an orientation that will help him to search for meaning and purpose. The nurse as a teacher can help the client to explore this search for meaning and purpose.

Another aspect of client education may include the identification of the nature of 'right relationship' with others. Morrison (1990) asserts that nursing concentration on this particular area can lead to improvements in clients' physical health. Educating clients to face up to defective relationships with others is an important aspect of spiritual care. Examples of defective relationships include: the denial of the death of a loved one; a lack of social concern; and an inability to accept hostility. The inability to experience the 'right relationship' is a known cause of spiritual distress (Morrison, 1989).

Learning is seen as a two-way process, in which the client experiences spiritual growth and the nurse achieves a greater spiritual awareness. Millison (1988) found in his study that nurses experienced heightened spirituality as a result of their work with ill people and that all nurses reported that they felt they received more in terms of spirituality than they were able to give. An increasing level of knowledge, insight and coping strategies relating to spirituality can be achieved through the process of sharing, as part of learning to cope with spirituality.

Summary

Skills development such as self-awareness, communication (listening), trust building, giving hope and client education is emphasised in this chapter. These skills, together with the previous introduction to the knowledge of spirituality, offer the reader a basis for the formulation of care plans related to spiritual care. The next two chapters introduce the reader to spiritual care as part of the nursing process.

References

Burnard P (1990) *Learning Human Skills: An Experiential Guide for Nurses.* 2nd edn. Heinemann Nursing, Oxford

Herth K (1990) Fostering hope in terminally ill people. *J Adv Nurs* **15**:1250–57

Millison MB(1988) Spirituality and caregiver, developing an underutilised facet of care. *Am J Hospice Care*, March/April: 37–44

Morrison R (1989) Spiritual health care and the nurse. *Nurs Standard* **4** (3/14): 28–29

Morrison R (1990) Spiritual health care and the nurse. *Nurs Standard* **5**(5): 34–35

Narayanasamy A (1998) Religious and Spiritual Needs of Older People. In: Pickering S, Thompson J (eds) *Promoting Positive Practice in Nursing Older People.* Baillière Tindal, London

Stuart GW, Sundeen SJ (1983) *Principles and Practice of Psychiatric Nursing.* CV Mosby, St Louis

6

The nursing process and spirituality

In previous chapters the significance of spirituality in the context of health care and skills necessary to provide spiritual care were addressed. Sufficient details were given to increase readers' confidence with regard to spiritual care. This chapter invites readers to consider a systematic approach to spiritual care using the nursing process. Although most nurses are well orientated to the nursing process, this chapter addresses it to emphasise that it is still an effective problem-solving tool which can be used systematically. According to Kratz (1979) the nursing process is:

> *A problem-solving approach to nursing that involves interaction with the patient, making decisions and carrying out nursing actions based on an assessment of an individual patient's situation. It is followed by an evaluation of the effectiveness of our action.*
>
> p. 3

The following four stages are included in the nursing process; assessment, planning, implementation and evaluation.

Assessment

Information obtained on religious needs alone is not enough for spiritual care. Such information does not allow us to go deeper into feelings about meaning and purpose of life, love and relationships, trust, hope and strength, forgiveness, expressions of beliefs and values. Also, this approach may lead to the assumption that a person who does not belong to a formal religion has no spiritual needs. As indicated earlier, the non-religious may have spiritual needs. The person who does not express obvious religious beliefs may still struggle with guilt, or lack meaning and purpose, or with need for love and relationships. On the other hand, a person who declares allegiance to a particular religion may not necessarily abide by the beliefs and practices of that religion.

Assumptions or conclusions should not be drawn about spiritual needs on the basis of patients' religious status.

The nurse must remain sensitive to verbal and non-verbal cues from patients when carrying out spiritual assessment. These cues might indicate a need to talk about spiritual problems.

Assessment of the patient's physical functioning may also provide valuable information for understanding their spiritual component. Such obvious considerations about patients, as their ability to see, hear, and move are important factors that may later determine the relevance of certain interventions. Also, psycho-social assessment data may serve a useful purpose in determining the patient's thought patterns, content of speech, affect (mood), cultural orientation, and social relationships. They may all provide the basis for identifying a need, or planning appropriate care, in conjunction with spiritual intervention.

The spiritual assessment guide (*Table 6.1*) may be useful for spiritual assessment. This guide includes general areas that can be appraised to derive data about spiritual concerns.

If patient/client declares religious beliefs/faith the assessment questions in *Table 6.2* could be added to the guide (*Table 6.1*).

Tubesing (1980) suggests a spiritual assessment procedure in which there are five questions to assess a person's spiritual outlook. Spiritual outlook embraces a person's faith, value, commitments, and ability to let go and to receive forgiveness from self and others. Tubesing's assessment questions for spiritual outlook are:

❖ What is the aim of life?

❖ What beliefs guide me?

❖ What is important to me?

❖ What do I choose to spend myself on?

❖ What am I willing to let go?

The presence of religious literature, for example, the Bible or Koran gives an indication of a patient's concerns about spiritual matters. Objects like religious requisites such as pictures, badges, pins, or articles of clothing are symbolic of a patient's spiritual expressions. A patient may keep a religious statue or Deity to carry out his religious rituals. Schedules can be used to carry out spiritual assessment by observations.

Table 6.1: Spiritual assessment guide

Needs	Questions	Assessment notes
Meaning and purpose	What gives you a sense of meaning and purpose? Is there anything especially meaningful to you now? Does the patient/client show any sense of meaning and purpose?	
Sources of strength and hope	Who is the most important person to you? To whom would you turn when you need help? Is there anyone we can contact? In what ways do they help? What is your source of strength and hope? What helps you the most when you feel afraid or need special help?	
Love and relatedness	How does patient relate to: family and relatives; friends; others; surrounding? Does patient/client appear peaceful? What gives patient/client peace?	
Self-esteem	Describe the state of client/patient's self-esteem How does patient/client feel about self?	
Fear and anxiety	Is patient/client fearful/anxious about anything?	
Anger	Is patient/client angry about anything? How does patient/client cope with anger? How does patient/client control this?	
Relation between spiritual beliefs and health	What has bothered you most being sick (or in what is happening to you?) What do you think is going to happen to you?	

Table 6.2: Religious needs assessment guide

Concept of God or deity	Is prayer (or meditation) important to you? How would you describe your God or what you worship?	
Spiritual practices	Do you feel your faith (or religion) is helpful to you? If yes, tell me more about it? If no, who would you like us to discuss with? Are there any religious practices that are important to you? Has being ill made any difference to your practice of praying (or meditation) or to your religious practices? Are there any religious books or symbols important to you? Is there anything that we could do to help with your religious practices?	

Non-verbal behaviour

1. Observe affect. Does the client's mood or attitude convey loneliness, depression, anger, agitation, or anxiety?
2. Observe behaviour. Does the client pray during the day? Does the client rely on religious music and reading material or other literature for solace?

Verbal behaviour

1. Does the client seem to complain out of proportion to his illness?
2. Does the client complain of sleeping difficulties?
3. Does the client ask for unusually high does of sedation or pain medication?
4. Does the client refer to God in any way?
5. Does the client talk about prayer, faith, hope or anything of a religious nature?
6. Does the client talk about church/place of worship/functions that are important in his life?

7.   Does the client express concern over meaning and direction of life?
8.   Does the client express concern over the impact of the illness on the meaning of life?

Interpersonal relationships

1.   Does the client have visitors or does he spend visiting hours alone?
2.   Are the visitors supportive or do they seem to leave the client feeling upset?
3.   Does the client have visitors from his place of worship?
4.   How does the client interact with staff and other clients?

Environment

1.   Does the client have a Bible or other religious reading material with him?
2.   Does the client wear religious medals, badges or pins?
3.   Does the client use religious articles such as statues in observing religious practices?
4.   Has the client received religious get-well cards?
5.   Does the client use personal pictures, artwork, or music to keep his spirits up?

Observations of the ways in which the patient relates with people, 'significant others' (people close to him, friends, and others who matter to him) may provide clues to the spiritual needs. The quality of interpersonal relationships can be ascertained. Does the patient welcome his visitors? Does their presence relax the patient or cause distress? Does he get visitors from the church or religious community? Observations of these factors can lead to conclusions about his social support system. The social system enables the patient to give and receive love and lack of such support may deprive the patient of this need and leave him distressed. The patient who has faith in God may feel estranged if he is cut off from his support network.

Observations of patient environment and significant objects/ symbols related to his religious practice may give evidence of his spirituality.

The other area of spiritual assessment includes attention to three factors: sense of meaning and purpose, means of forgiveness, and source of love and relationship. Observations and routine conversations with patients can lead to valuable information about each of these factors. Questions, as framed in *Table 6.1*, may be included when exploring with patients the meaning and purpose of life. Observations may include:

* how does the patient deal with other patients?
* does he ruminate over past behaviours or how he has been treated by other people?
* how does the patient respond to criticism?

If the patient responds with anger, hostility and blames others, these behaviours may suggest that he is unable to forgive himself and his consequent inability to tolerate anything that resembles criticism.

The spiritual assessment must also look at the patient's ability to feel loved, valued and respected by other people.

Planning

The planning of spiritual care requires careful attention. The data obtained from assessment must be interpreted in terms of spiritual needs and a care plan should be based on this information. The planning of spiritual care should include: respect for the patient's individuality; willingness of the nurse to get involved in the spirituality of the patient; use of therapeutic self; and the nurturing of the inner person, the spirit.

Assistance to meet spiritual needs should be given according to the indications of the individual, which may be unique and specific. If, for example, the patient is part of a church or religious group, and their effect on him appears positive, the nurse can strengthen this contact. A patient who is accustomed to practices such as meditating, praying, or reading the Bible or other religious books, should be given time and privacy. A visit by the patient's religious agent (pastor, rabbi, or others) can be arranged.

The nurse can make it easier for the patient to talk about spiritual beliefs and concerns, especially about how these relate to his illness. The nurse may need to help the patient in his struggle and search for meaning and purpose in life. On the other hand, if the patient is trying to find a source of hope and strength, then it can be used in planning care.

The other aspects of a nursing care plan may include comfort, support, warmth, self-awareness, empathy, non-judgemental listening and understanding. All these measures are the essence of a therapeutic relationship. An empathetic listener can do much to support a person who is spiritually distressed by being available when needed; for those patients suffering from loneliness, or those expressing doubts, fears and feelings of alienation, the presence of an empathetic person may have a healing effect.

For some patients a powerful source of spiritual care and comfort can be prayer, scripture and other religious readings. All these may alleviate spiritual distress. Prayers, as a source of help, would help a patient develop a feeling of oneness with the universe or a better relationship with God, comfort the patient, and help relieve spiritual distress. A particular prayer could be selected according to the patient's own style of comfort and needs. Although a nurse may not belong to the same faith as the patient, she could still support the patient in carrying out his spiritual beliefs.

Meditation, both religious and secular, can play an important role in enabling patients to relax, clear the mind, achieve a feeling of oneness with a Deity or the universe, promote acceptance of painful memories or decisions, and gather energy and hope that may help them to face spiritual distress.

The use of music gives an inspirational and calming effect. A wide variety of religious, inspirational and secular music may spiritually uplift a patient.

Implementation

Implementation of spiritual care is a highly skilful activity. It requires education and experience in spiritual care. Sufficient information is provided in this guide to extend the carer's knowledge of spirituality. In carrying out nursing actions related to spiritual needs, it is imperative that carers observe the following:

* do not impose personal beliefs (or lack of them) on patient or families
* respond to client's expression of need with a correct understanding of their background
* are sensitive to patient's signal for spiritual support.

If a nurse feels unable to respond to a particular situation of spiritual need, then he or she should enlist the services of an appropriate individual.

Nursing intervention should be based on an action which reflects caring for the individual. Caring signifies to the person that he or she is significant, and is worth someone taking the trouble to be concerned about them. Caring requires actions of support and assistance in growing. It means a non-judgemental approach and showing sensitivity to a person's cultural values, physical preference and social needs. It demands an attitude of helping, sharing, nurturing and loving. These actions fulfil the requirement of individualised spiritual care.

An understanding of the patient's unique beliefs and values or religious views is paramount in spiritual care. The carer must respect and understand the need for beliefs and practices even if these are not in accord with the nurse's faith. To allow a better understanding of the patient's spiritual needs, the carer must establish a rapport and trust which facilitates the patient to share those beliefs. The carer's own awareness of personal limitations in understanding these beliefs is paramount and he/she must seek outside help if necessary.

Nursing intervention should be based on a nurse-patient relationship which encourages the person to express views, fears, anxieties, and new understanding through creative acts, writing, poetry, music or art. Time for quiet reflection and opportunities for religious practices would enable the patient to develop a deeper understanding of life and a particular belief system.

The person who has no strong philosophical or religious belief may seek the opportunity to explore feelings, values and an understanding of life with another individual who is willing to give attention and time to discuss those areas of concern and share common human experiences. The nurse is the person who is most immediately available and receptive to the patient's thoughts and feelings for some patients. Certain patients may require their close friends, family or a religious person to share those thoughts and feelings. The nurse must remain sensitive to these needs and make the necessary arrangements. However, it must be remembered that spiritual growth is a life long process and the nurse who initiates spiritual care would have been a catalyst in the patient's goal to achieve eventual spiritual integrity and well-being.

Evaluation

Evaluation is an activity that involves the process of making a judgement about outcomes of nursing intervention. There are many indicators of spiritual outcomes, one of which is spiritual integrity. The person who has attained spiritual integrity, demonstrates this experience through a reality-based tranquillity or peace, or through the development of meaningful, purposeful behaviour, displaying a restored sense of integrity. O'Brien (1982) comments that the measure of spiritual care should establish the degree to which 'spiritual pain' was relieved. Another view offered by Kim *et al* (1984) suggest that spiritual care may be measured as the extent to which the 'life principle' was restored. The contents of patients' thoughts and feelings may also reflect spiritual growth through a greater understanding of life or an acceptance and creativity within a particular context.

As part of evaluation, the following questions may be helpful:

❖ Is the patient's belief system stronger?

❖ Do the patient's professed beliefs support and direct actions and words?

❖ Does the patient gain peace and strength from spiritual resources (such as prayer and minister's visits) to face the rigours of treatment, rehabilitation, or peaceful death?

❖ Does the patient seem more in control and have a clearer self-concept?

❖ Is the patient at ease in being alone? in having life plans changed?

❖ Is the patient's behaviour appropriate to the occasion?

❖ Has reconciliation of any differences taken place between the patient and others?

❖ Are mutual respect and love obvious in the patient's relationships with others?

❖ Are there any signs of physical improvement?

❖ Is there an improved rapport with other patients?

Summary

Effective spiritual care can be given through the systematic steps of the nursing process. Key assessment strategies and tools are indicated in this chapter. Data obtained from assessment strategies can be used for planning spiritual care. Useful guidance is provided for implementing spiritual care. Finally, evaluative measures are outlined in determining the patient's spiritual integrity.

References

Kim MJ, McFarland, SK, McLane AM (1984) *Pocket Guide to Nursing Diagnosis*. V Mosby, St Louis

Kratz CR (1979) *The Nursing Process*. Baillière Tindall, London

O'Brien ME (1982) Religious faith and adjustment to long-term haemodialysis. *J Religious Health* **21**: 68

Tubesing DA (1980) Stress: Spiritual outlook and health. *Specialised Pastoral Care J* **3**: 17

Annotated bibliography

Henley A, Scott J (1999) *Culture, Religion and Patient Care in Multi-Ethnic Society*. Age Concern, London

This book provides a comprehensive cover of cultural and religious issues and guidance material of patient care in a multi-ethnic society. The book addresses issues of race, ethnicity and anti-discriminatory practices. This book would be a good resource for practitioners wishing to develop deeper knowledge of cultural care.

McSherry W (2000) *Making Sense of Spirituality in Nursing Practice*. Churchill Livingstone, Edinburgh

The nursing process and spiritual care are addressed in chapter 4 of this book. Much useful guidance on spiritual care is given in this chapter. It also covers the ethical dimension of spiritual care.

Narayanasamy A, Daly P (1998) *Spiritual, Religious and Cultural Care: Resource Package*. Queen's Medical Centre, University of Nottingham, Nottingham

This package aims to provide nurses with some guidance on how to care for patients who, due to their cultural and spiritual needs, require sensitive consideration. The package is in an alphabetical order of faiths and beliefs with details related to cultural and spiritual aspects of nursing.

Ronaldson S (ed) (1997) *Spirituality: The Heart of Nursing*. Alismed Publications, Melbourne

This book addresses many issues central to spirituality and nursing care. A range of spiritual care as practised in a variety of settings is presented from the perspectives of leading academics and clinicians in Australia. In particular, readers will find chapters on spirituality, ageing and spiritual care in dementia valuable.

7

Putting the nursing process into action

In this chapter examples of specific care plans related to spiritual care are given. Although the focus of care plans outlined in this chapter is on spiritual care, it must be remembered that this forms only a part of a more comprehensive holistic care. In order to retain the spiritual focus of this book other aspects of care, although equally important, have been omitted.

Nursing care in acute illness

The spiritual needs of an individual during acute illness are intensified. In acute illness the spiritual needs may be expressed as a search for meaning in suffering and death; the patient may feel vulnerable in an impersonal and strange environment, and feel deprived of religious practices which may be a significant way of expressing individual faith.

The threat of imminent death may accentuate the need for greater spirituality. The fear of death is a universal response no matter how much an individual has prepared for it. The search for meaning becomes more apparent when death has been witnessed by an acutely ill patient who is also anticipating his own death. The non-believer may become bewildered by the absence of any clear meaning and purpose in life. The individual may experience anxiety, doubt, bitterness and fear of the unknown.

The person who feels estranged from his family and normal environment and suffering pain and fearing death while in hospital may experience the intense need for love and sources of strength and hope. These sources of strength and hope may include family and friends, carers and religious representatives. The person who has a strong religious faith, although relying on sources of strength indicated earlier, also depends ultimately on the love of his God, which may be seen as the greatest gift of all. For some, the belief that God is in ultimate control and can provide relief from suffering can be a great source of strength and comfort in enduring pain.

Case history one

Mr John Smith, aged 50, is married with two children and works as a self-employed builder and he is generally fit and healthy. John has been taken to A & E by the paramedics following an accidental fall from scaffolding. He has now been admitted to the CCU with suspected crushed vertebrae. Mr Smith appears very bewildered by this experience and has become very anxious and frightened. He is particularly preoccupied by financial worries. He has no strong religious convictions but belongs to the Church of England.

Nursing care plan (Mr John Smith)

Problem	Care plan
Search for meaning and purpose	Listen to patient's feelings and help him to explore meaning and purpose
Anxiety due to fear and financial worries	Explore with patient his thoughts and build his hope and expectations
Estrangement from family and environment	Help patient to review his life goals To recognise family as a source of strength

Case history two

Mrs Rani Patel, a Hindu, aged 25 years is admitted to A & E with threatened early labour and the scan indicates a boy. Rani was accompanied by her husband who appears extremely upset and anxious. They expressed their wishes to see a Hindu priest.

Nursing care plan (Mrs Rani Patel)

Problem	Care plan
Fear of losing baby	Reassurance that everything possible will be done to ensure safe pregnancy
Religious beliefs and practices	Contact their priest to visit patient Offer opportunity to carry out religious practices
Potential fear of letting her husband and family down if she loses the baby	Non-judgemental acceptance of patient's fear and feelings Facilitate husband and family to support patient that her health is paramount

Case history three

Mr Joseph Solomons is a 45-year-old businessman and belongs to the Jewish faith. He is married, but has no children. He works hard, leading a fairly stressful 'executive' type life, spending time away from home frequently. On one of his business trips Mr Solomons collapses and is admitted to the coronary care unit of the local hospital, with a suspected myocardial infarction. Mr Solomons finds it difficult in accepting change of diet and translating his Jewish dietary laws. He is also full of regrets about leading a stressful and busy life and blames himself for his illness. He also feels distressed that his chances of promotion are going to be affected because of illness and that he will be letting is family down. Mr Solomons is worried about his future.

Nursing care plan (Mr Joseph Solomons)

Problem	Care plan
Love and relationship	Enable patient to believe that his family's love for him is unconditional and not for what or who he is
Lack of time for self-reflection	Provide time and space for privacy and self-reflection
Finding a new source of meaning and purpose	Help patient explore meaning and purpose in life
Expressing faith, religious practices related to diet	Help patient re-affirm his faith and provide opportunity for expression of faith and to carry out religious practice Ensure that his dietary needs comply with Jewish law regarding food
Need for forgiveness; feelings of guilt and self-blame	Encourage patient to talk about his feelings Strengthen the closeness of family and enable them to act as his source of strength and hope Build his hope by helping him to review his plans and set new realistic goals for his future plans

Nursing care in chronic illness

Chronic illness may leave a person in a state of imbalance or disharmony of mind, body and spirit. Feelings of anger, sadness, guilt and anxiety are often common following a period of disorganisation and disruption. Despair and hopelessness may loom for the patient and his family. In their struggle with the impact of illness the patient and his family may feel separated from their usual support system. The patient's search for meaning in the disease may become apparent.

The patient's adaptation to his illness may mean new resolutions, losses to be acknowledged, roles and expectations to be re-defined. The illness not only has an impact upon the patient, but his family has to share its effects with him. Although individual reactions to illness differ, many people struggle as a result of the disharmony of mind, body and spirit. For some this means further spiritual growth or decline. The impact of an illness on a person compels him to turn in upon himself and re-consider his life (Tournier, 1974). The illness becomes a spiritual encounter as well as a physical and emotional experience. Research into coping strategies suggests that in chronic illness many subjects indicated that they gained strength from their spiritual life (Miller, 1983). This source of strength included a renewed faith in God, prayer, a sense of peace resulting from prayer, and a feeling God's love. Other strategies highlighted were meditation, receiving love and support from others, participating in church activities and a life review.

Narayanasamy (1996) provides a summary of the three strategies for the spiritual care of chronically ill patients as identified by Kitson (1985).

Nurse as comforter

As a comforter the nurse can be of great help by showing sensitivity to the patient's fear. This can be demonstrated in the way that the nurse respects the patient's dignity and personal integrity by recognising his/her humanity and worth.

The nurse can offer further comfort to patients by ensuring, if they wish, that they are able to worship according to their particular faith. Worship can be a personal or corporate activity on a regular basis. A nursing routine can be changed to provide patients with the privacy and time for prayer, meditation, scripture reading and other pursuits that promote their spiritual well-being.

Nurse as counsellor

A counselling approach is desirable in the nursing care of patients who require attention to spiritual needs. The nurse has to give time and attention to patients to support them in times of stress. This requires an awareness of patient's value systems, what support they use when facing stress, and the effects that the illness has on their social role. A counselling relationship is vital to support patients through frustration, anger and the feeling that they cannot cope any longer because of spiritual stress.

Nurse as challenger

In this role the nurse has to show patience and hope when working with spiritually distressed, chronically ill patients. A willingness to be part of the patient's experience during disruptions in their daily living pattern is vital. The nurse must avoid becoming rigid and viewing the problems arising from the illness as insurmountable. A sense of optimism is needed in what might be a depressing situation. This could be a challenging situation, even to the most experienced nurse.

Case history four

> Mr Robert Williams is aged 65, married and has a diagnosis of carcinoma of the lung. He is a foreman in a local factory. He is being treated with radiotherapy in an oncology ward. He frequently states: Why me? Why has God let this happen to me? He is angry and bitter towards life generally. He has a strong Christian faith.

Nursing care plan (Mr Robert Williams)

Problem	Care
Seeking purpose and meaning of life	Treat patient with respect and dignity Enable patient to review his plans and set new future plan
Needs love and forgiveness	Encourage patient to talk and help him ventilate his feelings, anger, bitterness and identify source of guilt Listen with empathy, without being judgemental Ask chaplain to visit, if patient wishes

Case history five

Mr Ali Khan, a 52-year-old Muslim has a long history of renal disease. He has a small family business. Mr Khan has been admitted to a medical ward following a history of uraemia, unconsciousness and dehydration. He is making a satisfactory recovery but remains very distressed, anxious and expresses feelings of loneliness. His family visit him regularly.

Nursing care plan (Mr Ali Khan)

Problem	Care plan
Spiritual distress due to lack of opportunity for prayer and religious practices	Build trust and relationship Listen and encourage patient to talk about his needs and faith Provide privacy and space for prayer and to read the Koran
Need for love and relationship due to separation from family	Encourage family to spend time with patient
Anxiety about not making plans for his family and business	Help patient to review his plans for his family Help patient to recognise his family as a source of strength

Nursing care in terminal illness

There is evidence to support spirituality as a significant human experience during terminal illness (Reed, 1987). In some instances a sense of spirituality acts as a resource in terminal illness. Spiritual well-being is related to low death fear, low discomfort, decreased loneliness, emotional adjustment, and positive death perspectives among terminally cancer and other seriously ill patients (Gibbes and Achterberg-Lawlis, 1978; Miller, 1985; O'Brien, 1982). The terminally ill patient facing death is likely to have the following spiritual needs: forgiveness/reconciliation, prayer/religious services, spiritual assistance at death and peace.

Forgiveness/reconciliation

There may be the feeling of unaccomplished relationship in that the patient may not have been granted forgiveness. The patient may seek ways and means of achieving reconciliation and this may reflect as wanting forgiveness and reconciliation with his God.

Prayer/religious services

Prayer, as indicated earlier, can be a source of comfort and strength. Religious services such as receiving sacraments, blessing of departures can all be very comforting to the patient and his family.

Spiritual assistance at death

The presence of a significant person, including a doctor or nurse and/or religious advisor at the bedside of a dying patient can be a very comforting spiritual assistance to the patient. This is an invaluable gift that can be given to a dying patient and his family.

Peace

Peace and tranquillity can be achieved through spirituality. All of the above needs contribute to spiritual well-being and this means attainment of peace and tranquillity.

Case history six

Mr Ronald Clarke, a 50-year-old teacher, is married with two teenage children. He has been admitted to hospital in the terminal stages of chronic myeloid leukaemia. He expresses a lot of anxiety about his illness, his wife and children. At times he was found to be frustrated and helpless and full of worries about the future of his family. Although Mr Clarke belongs to the Church of England he has no strong religious beliefs and tends to share humanist views. He likes classical music.

Nursing care plan (Mr Ronald Clarke)

Problem	Care plan
Anxiety due to separation from his family	Encourage patient to talk about his feelings
Frustration because of unachieved tasks in life and incomplete plans concerning security for his family	Provide time and space for quiet reflection Give hope by helping patient to revise his plans for the future with his family and set new goals
Helplessness because of illness	Build patient's hopes by uplifting his memories by helping patient to focus on previous achievements, happy events, etc Help patient to find his family as a source of strength
Needs opportunity for relaxation	Provide opportunities for listening to classical music

Case history seven

Mrs Pat Murphy, a 75-year-old widow, was admitted to hospital with terminal carcinoma. She has a strong faith and according to her family she attended a Catholic church frequently and she has been a source of strength to a lot of fellow church goers. In the course of her illness she began to feel agitated, alone and depressed.

Nursing care plan (Mrs Pat Murphy)

Problems	Care plans
Spiritual distress due to lack of meaning and purpose	Encourage patient to talk about feelings and help her to explore meaning and purpose
Loss of love and relatedness due to loss of contact with church and friends	Contact hospital chaplain to re-establish contact with church and friends
Anxiety about not being able to get to church	Offer opportunity for prayer Accompany patient to chapel if physical state allows Contact parish priest

Summary

In each of the above case studies the assessment strategies and tools suggested in *Chapter 6* can be applied. The care plans outlined in this chapter should not be treated as a precise protocol for spiritual care. Each individual is a unique person and should receive spiritual care as part of individualised patient care and this cannot be given from a pre-determined formula. The care plans arising from the short case histories are aimed as an illustration of the points raised earlier in this book. Case histories are chosen to demonstrate the diverse needs of patients from a variety of spiritual and religious backgrounds.

References

Gibbs HW, Achterberg-Lawlis J (1978) Spiritual values and death anxiety: Implication for counselling with terminal cancer patients. *J Counselling Psychology* **25**: 263–569

Kitson A (1985) Spiritual care in chronic illness. In: McGilloway O, Myco F (eds) *Nursing and Spiritual Care*. Harper Row, London: 142–145

Miller JF (1983) *Coping with Chronic Illness: Overcoming powerlessness*. FA Davis, Philadelphia

Miller JF (1985) Assessment of loneliness and spiritual well-being in chronically ill and healthy adults. *J Psychosoc Nurs* **1**(79): 79–85

Narayanasamy A (1996) Spiritual care of chronically ill patients. *Br J Nurs* **5**(5): 411–16

O'Brien ME (1982) Religious faith and adjustment to long-term haemodialysis. *J Religious Health* **2**(1): 68–72

Reed PG (1987) Spirituality and well-being in terminally ill hospitalised adults. *Res Nurs Health* **10**(5): 335–44

Tournier P (1974) *A Doctor's Case Book in the Light of the Bible*. SCM, London

8

Research and spiritual care

Introduction

No book on spiritual care can conclude without a section on research in this area of nursing and this book is no exception. Moreover, readers wishing to research into spiritual care may find this chapter useful and for many it might be the starting point. Concepts related to spirituality are emerging as a result of growing research. Several assumptions are made on the basis of research into the understanding of spirituality. Some of the research findings and assumptions are given in this chapter.

Spirituality: In pursuit of conceptual and theoretical unity

The contribution of nursing literature in the pursuit of conceptual and theoretical unity has been steady and consistent. Apart from the earlier interest in the topic of nursing circles in North America, although many of these come from a more evangelical stance, the UK sources are emerging to make an impact in acknowledging the importance of the spiritual dimension in nursing. In the eighties of the last century Simsen (1986) began to address spirituality as a nursing dimension, however, other writers like Burnard (1987), Narayanasamy (1999a, 1993), Bown and Williams (1993), Harrison (1993), Bradshaw (1994), Ross (1996), Oldnall (1996) and McSherry and Draper (1998) soon followed with their contribution to this paradigm in nursing. In a recent paper, McSherry and Draper (1998) developed a debate in exploring the concept of spirituality as applied to nursing. In this debate these authors raised issues surrounding the complex and diverse nature of spirituality, and drew the conclusion that spirituality defies definitions, as pointed out in chapter one of this book.

Narayanasamy (1999b) charts the historical development of spirituality in his paper, 'Learning spiritual dimensions of care from a historical perspective'. This paper charts the spiritual influences of nursing in ancient civilisations like Egypt, Mesopotamia, China, Palestine, India, Greece and Rome. It also examines the influence of Christianity on nursing during the Middle Ages, Renaissance, eighteenth, nineteen and twentieth centuries. Finally, the emerging theories of nursing and their position on spirituality (including those of humanists) are reviewed and commented. In the light of the review of historical development of spirituality in nursing, the paper concludes that there is scope to develop educational programmes to better equip nurses to meet patients' spiritual needs.

Nurses' awareness of spiritual needs

In a study into nurses' awareness of patient's spiritual concerns, Highfields and Cason (1983) found that despite the fact that nursing learning opportunities include content about client's physical and psychological needs, information about spiritual needs is often omitted. The study found that only patients' expressions of specific beliefs and practices were associated with the spiritual dimension by nurses. Also, respondents thought behaviours and conditions related to spirituality occurred infrequently among patients.

The need for nurses to increase their spiritual awareness is stressed by Clifford and Gruca (1987). They write: 'Nurses need to start with self-examination of their own spiritual values and attitudes' (p. 332). Nurses who witness and share in their clients' distress first hand are likely to become involved in spiritual care. Likewise, in Scotland, Ross (1996) found this to be the case in her study of nurses' perception of spiritual care. Montgomery (1991), in her study of 'The care-giving relationship: paradoxical and transcendent aspects', also observes that nurses who allow themselves to be close to patients actually experience, on some level, the patient's healing, or the positive effects of their caring. David Lewis (1995), in a study of nurses in a large hospital in Leeds, found that many of them spoke of their first encounter with spiritual or religious experiences from their working with patients.

In a more recent study, Narayanasamy and Owen (2001) found that confusion exists among nurses over the notion of spirituality and their role related to spiritual care. Some nurses interpret spirituality as being to do with religion. A variety of approaches to spirituality emerged from 115 critical incidents provided by nurses who participated in the study. The researchers categorised these as 'personal', 'procedural', 'culturalist' or 'evangelical'. Nurses who took a 'personal' approach were willing to give time and personal attention to patients and engage in all aspects of patient care. Their approach was characteristic of therapeutic relationships and communications, treating patients as individuals and partners in care. Those who took a 'procedural' approach were systematic, impersonal and routine orientated. They tended to stereotype patients in terms of religious and cultural labels. Nurses who utilised a 'culturalist' approach responded to patients and their families with a greater degree of sensitivity in addressing their cultural and spiritual needs. Those taking an 'evangelical' approach tended to share similar religious backgrounds with patients. They made great efforts to re-affirm patients' faith, especially if they appeared to be lapsed Christians. Nurses believed that reaffirmation of patients' faith may help with healing.

Furthermore, the findings of this study suggest that there was an overwhelming consensus that patients' faith and trust in nurses produces a positive effect on patients and their families, and nurses themselves derive satisfaction from the experiences of giving spiritual care. In this respect, according to this study, spiritual care interventions promote a sense of well-being in nurses as well as being a valuable part of total patient care.

Spiritual needs of patients

In a survey into spiritual needs, Stallwood (1975) found that many patients would appreciate help in meeting their spiritual needs from a nurse who was available to listen and then personally intervene or refer to the appropriate spiritual counsellor. A further conclusion of this study was that a nurse should also be sensitive to the patient who believes that spiritual care is not the nurse's role and the patient who desires no help at all.

Burnard (1987) suggests that spirituality is a basic human need and its absence results in spiritual distress. He states:

> *Spiritual distress is the result of the inability to invest in life with meaning. It can be demotivating, fearful and can cause anguish to the sufferer.*
>
> p. 377

He argues that counselling is one approach that can help patients overcome spiritual distress.

In a descriptive study into spiritual needs, Martin and Burrows (1976) found that females expressed more spiritual needs than males. Similarly, when Hay (1987) surveyed the general population into their awareness of spirituality, he found that 41 per cent of the women interviewed talked of such experiences, compared with 31 per cent of the men. Martin and Burrows also found that the clergy is the preferred body with whom patients prefer to speak about spiritual needs; concerns and kindness were expected from nurses by patients; and nurses were expected to listen to patients.

Nurse education and spirituality

Chadwick (1973) found in her studies that many nurses were aware of the presence of spiritual needs in at least some of their patients, but expressed that they would like further education in meeting spiritual needs in patients. This is consistent with Simsen's (1986) assertion that there is little practical guidance available for nurses who wish to understand a patient's spiritual needs and resources.

In a similar vein, Piles (1986) found that the role of practising professional registered nurses for providing spiritual care was based on an educational preparation for such a role. A significant number of those questioned felt inadequately prepared to perform such roles, and many recommended that 'spiritual care' content be included in every basic nursing programme. In a more recent study of nurses' awareness and educational preparation in meeting patients' spiritual needs, Narayanasamy (1993) found that nurses gave two reasons for being unable to give spiritual care. Firstly, nurse education does not adequately prepare nurses to provide spiritual care. Secondly, spiritual care is seen as the realm of hospital chaplains/religious representatives. However, caution is needed in generalising from the findings of this study as it was based on a small sample (n=33).

In the UK Ross (1996) found that nurses felt the need for further professional preparation to help them to be effective in providing spiritual care. Although Ross proposes tentative guidelines for spiritual care education, she is less than clear about how this could be achieved in reality. Apart from the guidelines, Ross does not emphasise the significance of communication skills and assessment procedures as part of the approach to spiritual care needs. However, she acknowledges in the study's report that further investigative research into the effectiveness of nurse education in meeting patients' spiritual needs is required.

Narayanasamy (1999c) offers the ASSET Model for actioning spirituality and spiritual care education and training in nursing. This model evolved as a response to the need for clearer directions in the delivery of spiritual care education. The model offers workable definitions and theoretical perspectives rooted in theology, socio-biology and existentialism. Apart from theoretical perspectives, this model provides some directions in the development of skills for spiritual care, including self-awareness and value clarifications, communication skills, competence in assessment, planning, implementing and evaluation. It offers further hints on enhancing quality of care, spiritual integrity and healing and relief from spiritual pain. Readers are requested to refer to this paper for extensive details on above issues. It should prove to be a useful model for spiritual care education and training in practice.

Spirituality and mental illness

According to Peterson and Nelson (1987) in mental illness spiritual distress is related to two phenomena: the inability to practice rituals and the conflict between religious or spiritual beliefs and prescribed health regimes. Both authors suggest that mentally ill clients often struggle with finding a source of meaning and purpose in their lives. The need for forgiveness is a frequent problem in mentally ill clients. Unmet needs in relation to forgiveness result in guilt and resentment. Narayanasamy (2000) uses case histories to suggest how spiritual needs of mental health clients may be met. Clear directions on the skill development for mental health nurses are provided to help nurses to be effective in spiritual care interventions.

Spirituality and chronic illness

In a similar vein, Soeken and Carson (1987) express that a disharmony of mind, body and spirit is a product of the crisis brought on by chronic illness. A period of disorganisation and disruption takes place at the initial stage of adaptation to chronic illness. These authors state: 'Following the initial diagnosis of the disease, feelings of sadness, anger, guilt, and anxiety are not uncommon' (p 604).

A North American study by Miller (1983) suggests that in chronic illness many subjects indicated that they gained strength from the spiritual life. The source of strength included a renewal of faith in God, prayer, a sense of peace resulting from prayer and a feeling of God's love. In another study, Miller (1985) compared the spiritual well-being of rheumatoid arthritis patients with that of healthy adults. Although there was no significant differences between the groups in the level of existential well-being (that is, a sense of life purpose and satisfaction), those with arthritis reported a significantly higher level of religious well-being, defined as a sense of well-being in relation with God.

In a qualitative study of spiritual care of chronically ill patients Narayanasamy (1995) found that crises in individuals' lives (ie. diagnosis of chronic illnesses) evoked a need for spiritual support. Patients resorted to various spiritual coping mechanisms as a way of coping with crises such as illnesses. Some patients used bargaining strategies for a miracle cure and strength was sought by making a plea to God through prayer. Some patients found that their faith in God was a source of hope in coping with the crisis brought on by illness. However, unless prompted, feelings related to spirituality/ spiritual responses were kept private. The researcher's conversational style of interviews prompted patients to talk freely about their spiritual needs.

Furthermore, the findings of this study suggest that patients' spiritual needs were not met adequately by nurses for the following reasons. Firstly, nurses were seen as 'too busy' to fulfil a function in spiritual care, although their role in this was acknowledged. Secondly, some nurses were perceived as having little or no understanding of spirituality themselves and were therefore not seen as useful for spiritual care.

Spirituality and children

Edward Robinson (1977) recounts in his book, *The Original Visions* that many children experience what could be described as spiritual experiences (mystical experiences). Likewise, Sommer (1989) suggests children experience spirituality as much as adults. He writes:

> *Who but children can show us so much about what it meant to be human, revealing that all of us are rather fragile creatures, struggling for life, trying to fulfil our potential, expressing our uniqueness, living in relationship with God.*
>
> p. 225

Hay (1987) suggests that the socialisation/conditioning process represses their innate propensity to experience and express their spirituality. Furthermore, Kenny (1999) points out that Sommer's association of children's spirituality with those of adults is flawed thinking. He argues that this flawed thinking is due to the paucity in the literature on children's spirituality. In spite of this criticism, Kenny fails to deliver a clear alternative to Sommer's perspectives on children's spirituality. He leaves it for paediatric nurses to reconstruct children's spirituality based on observations of their linguistic expressions and beliefs associated with their spirituality and religion. Further research is needed to clear the fog that covers children's spirituality presently.

Spirituality and stress

According to Labun (1988) there are interrelationships among the physical, emotional and spiritual aspects of a person. She states:

> *... stress in the emotional or spiritual aspects may result in a change in physical functioning.*
>
> p. 315

Altered spiritual integrity is reflected as experiences such as spiritual pain, alienation, anxiety, guilt, anger, loss and despair. Spiritual pain can leave a person very distressed and disturbed. Spiritual pain is an experience defined as an individual's perception of hurt or suffering connected with that part of his person that seeks to transcend the realm of the material. It is an experience of a deep sense of hurt stemming from feelings of loss or separation from one's God or Deity, a sense of personal guilt or sinfulness before God or man, a lasting condition of loneliness of spirit (Labun, 1988).

Spirituality and terminal illness

A study conducted by Reed (1987) revealed that a higher percentage of terminally ill patients had experienced a change and developed an increased level of spirituality than non-terminally ill or healthy adults. This is consistent with other research findings in which spiritual manifestations of transcendence are significant to the experience faced by the dying patients (Augustine and Kalish, 1975; Bascom, 1984; Hood and Morris, 1983; Klass and Gordon, 1978–79; Lifton, 1979). Aldridge (1987) stresses the need for a co-ordinated approach to the care of the dying and their families. He suggests that an integrated approach is needed that takes account of the dying person and the family's physical, psychological, spiritual and social dimensions of lives. With regard to the family's spirituality, Aldridge points out that the following should be given consideration: feelings of loss, alienation and abandonment; understanding suffering; accepting dependency; handling anger and frustration; forgiving others; discovering peace; discussing death; grieving and planning the funeral.

Summary

Spirituality as a concept is becoming established as research makes explicit many of its previously unknown facets. Theories and models of spirituality are emerging as a result of these research findings. There is now enough research evidence to suggest that spiritual care has a significant place in nursing. It is beyond any doubt that meeting the spiritual needs of patients is a fundamental part of holistic care.

References

Aldridge D (1987) Families, cancer and dying. *Fam Pract* **14**(3): 212–218

Augustine MJ, Kalish RA (1975) Religion, transcendence, and appropriate death. *J Transpersonal Psychol* **7**(1): 1–13

Bascom GS (1984) Physical, emotional, and cognitive care of dying patients. *Bull Menninger Clin* **48**: 351–356

Bown J, Williams A (1993) Spirituality and nursing: a review of the literature. *J Adv Health Nurs Care* **2**: 41–66

Bradshaw A (1994) *Lighting the Lamp; the Spiritual Dimension of Nursing Care*. Scutari, London

Burnard P (1987) Spiritual distress and the nursing response: Theoretical consideration and counselling skills. *J Adv Nurs* **12**: 377–382

Chadwick R (1973) Awareness and preparedness of nurses to meet spiritual needs. In: Shelly A, Fish S (eds) *Spiritual Care: The Nurse's Role*. InterVarsity Press, Illinois:177–178

Clifford BS, Gruca JA (1987) Facilitating spiritual care. *Rehabilitation Nurs* **12**(6): 331–333

Harrison J (1993) Spirituality and nursing practice. *J Clin Nurs* **2**: 211–217

Hay D (1987) *Exploring Inner Space*. Mowbray, London

Highfields MF, Cason C (1983) Spiritual needs of patients: Are they recognised? *Cancer Nurs*, June: 187–192

Hood RW, Jr, Morris RJ (1983) Toward a theory of death transcendence. *J Scientific Study Religion* **22**: 353–365

Kenny G (1999) Assessing children's spirituality: what is the way forward? *Br J Nurs* **8**(1): 28–32

Klass D, Gordon A (1978–79) Varieties of transcending experience at death: a videotape based study. *OMEGA* **9**: 19–36

Labun E (1988) Spiritual Care: an element in nursing care planning. *J Adv Nurs* **13**: 314–320

Lewis D (1985) All in good faith. *Nurs Times* **18**(24): 40

Lifton RJ (1979) *The Broken Connection*. Simon and Schuster, London

Martin C, Burrows C (1976) Spiritual needs of patient study. In: Shelly A, Fish S (eds) (1988) *Spiritual Care*: The Nurses Role. InterVarsity Press, Illinois: 160–76

McSherry W, Draper P (1998) The debates emerging from the literature surrounding the concept of spirituality as applied to nursing. *J Adv Nurs* **27**: 683–681

Miller JF (1985) Assessment of loneliness and spiritual well-being in chronically ill and healthy adults. *J Prof Nurs* **11**: 78–85

Miller JF (1983) *Coping with Chronic Illness*. FA Davies, Philadelphia

Montgomery CL (1991) The care-giving relationships. Paradoxical and transcendent aspects. *J Transpersonal Psychol* **23**(3): 91–105

Narayanasamy A, Owen J (2001) A critical incident study of nurses' responses to the spiritual care of their patients. *J Adv Nurs* **33**(4): 446–55

Narayanasamy A (2000) Spiritual care and mental health competence. In: Thompson T, Mathias P (eds) *Lyttle's Mental Health and Disorder*. Baillière Tindall, London: 305–324

Naryanasamy A (1999a) A review of spirituality as applied to nursing. *Int J Nurs Stud* **36**: 117–125

Narayanasamy A (1999b) Learning spiritual dimensions of care from a historical perspective. *Nurse Educ Today* **19**: 386–395

Narayanasamy A (1999c) ASSET: A model for actioning spirituality and spiritual care education and training in nursing. *Nurse Educ Today* **19**: 274–285

Narayanasamy A (1995) Research in brief: spiritual care of chronically ill patients. *J Clin Nurs* **4**: 397–400

Narayanasamy A (1993) Nurses' awareness and preparedness in meeting their patients spiritual needs. *Nurse Educ Today* **13**: 196–201

Oldnall AS (1996) A critical analysis of nursing: meeting the spiritual needs of patients. *J Adv Nurs* **23**(1): 138–144

Peterson E, Nelson K (1987) How to meet your clients' spiritual needs. *J Psychosoc Nurs* **25**(5): 34–38

Piles C (1986) *Spiritual Care: Role of Nursing Education and Practice: a needs survey for curriculum development*. Unpublished doctoral dissertation, St Louis University

Reed PG (1987) Spirituality and well-being in terminally ill hospitalised adults. *Res Nurs Health* **10**(5): 335–344

Robinson E (1977) *The Original Vision*. Religious Research Unit, Manchester College, Oxford

Ross LA (1996) Teaching spiritual care to nurses. *Nurse Educ Today* **16**: 38–43

Simsen B (1986) The spiritual dimension. *Nurs Times*, 26 Nov: 41–42

Soeken KL, Carson VJ (1987) Responding to the spiritual needs of the chronically ill. *Nurs Clin North Am* **22**(3): 603–611

Sommer DR (1989) The spiritual needs of dying children, issues comprehensive. *Pediatr Nurs* **12**(2–3): 225–233

Stallwood J (1975) Spiritual dimensions of nursing practice. In: Beland I, Passos J (eds) *Clinical Nursing*. Macmillan, Basingstoke

Index